Life-Arc Teaching Tales

Life-Arc Teaching Tales

John Zeugner

RESOURCE *Publications* • Eugene, Oregon

LIFE-ARC TEACHING TALES

Copyright © 2015 John Zeugner. All rights reserved. Except for brief quotations in critical publications or reviews, no part of this book may be reproduced in any manner without prior written permission from the publisher. Write: Permissions, Wipf and Stock Publishers, 199 W. 8th Ave., Suite 3, Eugene, OR 97401.

Resource Publications
An Imprint of Wipf and Stock Publishers
199 W. 8th Ave., Suite 3
Eugene, OR 97401

www.wipfandstock.com

ISBN 13: 978-1-4982-1900-6

Manufactured in the U.S.A.   04/03/2015

"The Revolutionaries," appeared originally in *The South Carolina Review* (June, 1971)
"The Rescue," appeared, in slightly different form, in *Southern Humanities Review* (Fall, 1969)

For Emily, Max, and Laura Ruth

"Any subject can be taught effectively in some intellectually honest form to any child at any stage of development."

—JEROME BRUNER

"Most people learn most of the time when they do whatever they enjoy; most people are curious and want to give meaning to whatever they come in contact with; and most people are capable of personal, intimate intercourse with others unless they are stupefied by inhuman work or turned off by schooling."

—IVAN ILLICH

Contents

Part I: Headwaters

1 The Who and With Stories for Certain Children | 3
   Preface
      The Deer Who Stood Very Still
      The Girl with the Endless Hair
      The Boy with the Lonely Vest
      The Pitcher Who Never Threw
      The Surfer Who Rode a Long, Long Time

2 A Citation | 25

3 The Revolutionaries | 35

Part II: Mid-Stream

4 The Rescue | 57

5 Accidents of Lust | 73

6 The Toughest Bar in Worcester | 88

7 We Say 4 Is Bigger than, Larger than, More than 3 | 105

Part III: At the Falls

8 The Point Of The Hook | 117

9 Nothing in Newark | 130

10 Near Death in Venice | 144

Part I

Headwaters

1

The Who and With Stories for Certain Children

Preface

AMONG THE MYRIAD MOTIVATIONS for writing fiction here's one that doesn't often get itemized: the Vice Principal explained to the novice substitute, "Your last class of sixth graders is very low. Very low. You'll have to work very hard to keep control. Very hard. Two previous substitutes quit, the last one simply walked away before the bell. You'll have to plan activities very thoroughly, and keep them very short, very changing. And remember when they're done with you, the day is over. Remember that, it will sustain you."

My first encounter with this last class, all 31 of them, was scalding. I tried a spelling bee and actually had two lines formed along the walls, before mutual screaming commenced, then mutual recriminations, pencil hurlings, and desk shovings. I was thankful the class was held in a separate "modular unit" so the fury and fisticuffs apparently didn't carry all the way to the main building. But that was only temporary respite. Above the rage I managed to bellow "Okay! Okay! Return to your seats and I'll tell you a story."

That prospect somehow tamed the tumult and soon enough most of them were seated and anticipatory. I sensed the story would have to center around what I thought would be their natural interests, with wild turns toward the unexpected, plus whiffs of violence and distant gore. Of course the central characters would have to be sixth graders, so I hatched a story of two Bills, both sixth graders, who found a way to permanently paralyze a deer.

As I hysterically spun out the story (each event tracking the remorselessly slow giant clock over the exit door to the module) the room became quiet, and I had the disturbing revelation that they were following what I was saying. Were they finding coherence in what I was shoveling toward them? It seemed so. I piled on the grisly details, culminating in the savage demise of the deer. I finished just as the bell rang.

"That was pretty stupid," one of them said, exiting. "I hope tomorrow's a better story." It was the first time in my life when telling a story I made up, worked, in the sense it got a result I desperately needed. At the same time it brought unbelievable pressure to hatch the next story in the one empty period I had just before that last toughest class of the day. Invariably I ended up using a huge abandoned Royal typewriter in the teachers' lounge to pen, in forty-five sweat-filled minutes, the next story to ensure the blessed silence that all successful substitutes are expected to generate. Hang the learning—maintain the quiet and get called back tomorrow.

In the two weeks I was at that elementary school I ginned up about a dozen stories, each one with a title using "who" or "with." Years later I put them together (still sweating with residue fear) under the title "The Who and With Stories for Certain Children." I hoped to publish and sell them as a sort of very German, very sick, collection of sadistic fairy tales. But an editor at Harcourt returned them with the comment they seemed to come directly out of my unconscious and as such shouldn't be inflicted on the reading public. I had even found an illustrator for the first story about the Bills, but I agreed with the editor's assessment and put them away. What follows are five arbitrarily selected ones originally typed in desperation to quiet some "very low" sixth graders.

THE DEER WHO STOOD VERY STILL

Gabriel's father, a giant of a deer, with antlers that almost touched the sun, had been killed a long time ago because he jumped when he should have stood still. Gabriel had learned that lesson well. Whenever the hunters came with their red coats and their red eyes, whenever the season of shouts and guns started, Gabriel, now a full grown stag himself, always stood very, very still. It always worked. The hunters, bursting out of the woods aimed their powerful rifles at Gabriel and then lowered them slowly.

"It must be a statue," they always said.

"Don't be ridiculous," someone always answered. "Whoever heard of a statue way out here in the woods? Go ahead and shoot."

"You ever see a deer that would let you walk right up to him?" the hunters always answered, and then they would walk right up to Gabriel and stroke him, and lean on him, and remark how lifelike his coat seemed, though they were sure it was only metal, or maybe stone, or maybe some combination of both.

And so Gabriel passed five hunting seasons that way. Whenever the hunters came, Gabriel froze right up—never moving so much as an eyelash, and then the hunters gathered around him and allowed that they had never seen such a strange thing: a statue of a deer right in the middle of the forest, as if the city had decided to build a park and then forgotten about it. And then, of course, the hunters went and looked for deer that eventually died because they jumped when they should have stood very still.

And so at the beginning of each hunting season Gabriel always said goodbye to his proud stag friends and their lovely doe wives, because he said, "Since you will not stand still, since you will jump, you therefore will probably be killed." It was a sad time.

Then in the sixth hunting season something terrible happened to Gabriel. He had begun well enough. Three times he had let surprised hunters walk up to him and remark about his coat and then go away. And it was not because he was over confident, cocky about his play acting (Gabriel was never that sure of himself)—no, it was not being too big for his hooves that got Gabriel into a terrible mess. No. Rather, it was because something new happened. Something Gabriel could not have been prepared for. Something that just was not thinkable.

The hunters always told the story of the statue deer when they got back to their homes. But of course some hunters in their stories put Gabriel in one part of the forest and other hunters put Gabriel somewhere else. It never occurred to the hunters that Gabriel, the statue deer, could move. Why should such a thought ever occur to the hunters? Now, two hunters each had a son named Bill, and the two Bills often talked about the mysterious statue deer that their fathers put at opposite ends of the forest. The two Bills vowed they would find the statue deer and would mark him plainly for all to see. Then there would never be another argument about where the deer was. So the two Bills followed their fathers into the forest and tried to find Gabriel.

Now Gabriel was prepared for hunters but not for young boys. When the hunters came, he naturally froze right up, and sure enough, the hunters passed him by. They clattered off into the brush and Gabriel began the long process of relaxing all over—-for it was quite a feat to become a statue, quite a tiring feat. Just as Gabriel had managed to get all the movement back into his hind legs, he heard a shifting in the woods behind him. He looked around, saw two boys coming at him. He thought, was this the time to jump or was this the time to stand still? He couldn't decide. He tried to think it through, but he got confused, and so finally he decided to do the thing that had always worked. He stood still, very, very still—-even though it was an awkward position with his head turned back toward his tail.

The two Bills were overjoyed.

"Look, Bill, we've found the statue deer," Bill said.

"Yes, Bill, we've finally done it," Bill answered. "I'll wait here. You go back and get the stuff."

The other Bill left and a strange feeling of numbing coldness came into Gabriel. What did the boys mean by "stuff"? Gabriel soon found out, for Bill came back with two large cans that made him wobble as he ran. And two large brushes. The boys started to work.

Gabriel thought, I should have jumped when I stood still. I should have, for he felt the heavy white liquid being brushed onto his hind legs. I should have jumped thought Gabriel, as the heavy stiff white liquid was slathered across his back and stroked down on his stomach. I should have jumped when I stood still, Gabriel repeated in his mind as the boys began coating his front legs. But it was of course too late. It would have taken too long for Gabriel to unfreeze. Oh, I've made the wrong decision, Gabriel thought. After all these years of right decisions and now the wrong one. He could feel the liquid firming up around his body. Was it paint or cement? He sniffed but couldn't tell. It was cold and frightening and Gabriel knew he could not move if he wanted to. And then the boys began applying the stuff to his head. Gabriel felt the cold liquid nestle on his forehead and then streak icily down his nose and he thought, in a second I'll have to close my eyes for they mean to cover my eyes

And one of the Bills said, "Shall we do the eyes?" And the other Bill said, "Yes, of course! It wouldn't look right if we didn't do the eyes." And so they came with their brushes to do the last part of Gabriel. Gabriel sighed deeply, regretted his decision, and then closed his eyes, to be sealed up forever.

Part I: Headwaters

THE GIRL WITH THE ENDLESS HAIR

Because her daughter's hair had grown all around the house, Mrs. Fish each day had to use a hedge clipper to get out of her front door. It was embarrassing. Mr. And Mrs. Fish had sent Ellen to bed a week before because she had been nasty and talked back to them. The next morning Ellen's hair had slithered out from under bedroom door.

"Are you in there, Ellen?" Mrs. Fish had asked.

"Yes," Ellen replied.

"Well, pull your hair in and come down here."

"I can't, "Ellen answered. "It's filled up the whole room and besides, it's lovely hair, lovely, lovely hair."

"Oh," Mrs. Fish said, and hurried downstairs. She sat quietly in the den and rubbed her hands. Mr. Fish would know what to do. But all Mr. Fish said when came downstairs was, "You probably think it's attractive. Lovely indeed!" Then he went to work.

All that day Ellen's hair grew and grew. It slithered down the stairs and apparently out of her bedroom window too, because Mr. Fish, when he came home that night, had to use a sickle to get into the garage. "You probably think it's attractive," Was all Mr. Fish said, and then he sat down and read his paper.

"Do you realize that Ellen's hair has filled up the whole upstairs? Do you realize we'll have to sleep in the den tonight? Do you? Mrs. Fish was extremely upset, but Mr. Fish only read the paper and asked about dinner.

"She's your daughter," Mrs. Fish finally said over a bowl of cream of mushroom soup. "We have to do something," Mrs. Fish said. "Ellen hasn't eaten in a week. We have to care about her."

"Care about her when her hair is strangling our lovely home? The home we've worked for all our lives. Care about her indeed."

So Mr. And Mrs. Fish stopped caring about Ellen and began to worry about their home. That night they took the hedge clipper and sheared for two hours at the clump of massive hair which was now sprawling into the living room. Finally, tired and disgusted, they slammed the door of the den and went to bed. In the morning they couldn't move the door of the den open. Using his razor Mr. Fish slashed an opening through the hair over the outside of the den window and went to work as usual, though he muttered heavily at the traffic. When he came home, Mrs. Fish was in the street and so were several neighbors with hoses and shovels, scythes, axes and saws. The whole Fish house seemed to a clump of hair which very rapidly was engulfing the neighborhood.

The hair already covered the Ransom house and seemed to be over-curling the Fosdick garage.

"You probably think it's attractive," Mr. Fish and sat in his car reading his paper.

"You just can't sit there," Mrs. Fish said, really beside herself. "You daughter is somewhere in there. Do something!"

Mr. Fish shrugged and put his paper down. He stood up on the car hood. "Ellen!" he shouted. "Ellen! Can you hear me?" The neighbors turned off their hoses, put down their scythes.

"Yes, came a faint muffled voice. "Yes."

"Ellen, this is your father. Please stop your hair from growing. Ellen, please stop your hair from growing."

There was a pause and then Mr. Fish was sure he heard a little tiny laugh and then Ellen said, "I will not. It's my hair and it's lovely. Do you hear? Lovely, lovely hair."

Mr. Fish got down off the car. "There's your answer," he said.

The neighbors picked up the hoses and the scythes and set to work again. But Ellen's hair was growing faster than they could work.

"We'll have to go to the other side of town and get some help. This is really spreading," someone said.

"Good," the others agreed. "We'll get some help."

But on the other side of town no one cared much one way or the other about Ellen's hair. "That's your problem," they said. "We have enough to do over here. There are a lot of loose dogs over here, for example."

"Don't you see," Mrs. Fish said, "It's just a matter of time. Soon my daughter's hair will be here."

Part I: Headwaters

"Perhaps that will help us with the stray loose dogs," they answered.

Of course, in a week they changed their feelings, for Ellen's hair, relentless and brown, had gobbled up the whole town. Soldiers from the state stood guard on the edge of the town and with flame throwers tried to hold back Ellen's advancing hair. But it was no good. "We'll have to go to the capital," the soldiers said. "This job is too big for us. We're losing too many men already."

But at the capital the legislators said, "Don't bother us with some child's hair. We have tremendous national problems. Taste the air you breathe. Go ahead and taste."

The soldiers tasted.

"You like that?"

The soldiers shook their heads.

"Of course you didn't like that. Now, after that aren't you ashamed of bringing your childish hair problem here to the capital?"

"Don't you see," Mrs. Fish said, "that it's just a matter of time?"

Mr. Fish added, "They probably think it's attractive."

Of course, in a week the legislators were beside themselves. Ellen's hair had swarmed all over the country, swarmed everywhere, gnarling up traffic in the cities and tractors on the farms, had reached down into subways, blocking them, and smothered all the railroads, was, in fact, snuffing out every bare spot on the continent. The legislators had taken to the air. They met in helicopters and finally decided that there was no choice. They had to use the ultimate weapon, fire. Ellen's hair would have to be burned off the face of the earth. There was no other way.

Mr. Fish begged for a chance to talk to his daughter, so the legislators flew him across the top of his old home.

"Ellen," he shouted, "Ellen, can you hear me?"

"Yes," came a strong reply. "And stop shouting. I'm not deaf."

"Ellen, I beg you. Stop your hair from growing. This is the last chance for us. The legislators will have to use fire. Stop your hair, please! Remember we love you. Save yourself. Stop your hair from encircling the earth."

Mr. Fish listened hard and, sure enough, again came that strange laugh and then Ellen said, "I will not. It's lovely, lovely hair."

Mr. Fish looked sad. He nodded at the chief legislator. "Use fire," he said. "She's my daughter and I love her, but use fire. Go ahead. Get it over with."

The chief legislator radioed the command and within minutes tons of fire dropped from the sky. Ellen's hair blazed forth filling the night air with orange, searing strips and scales of yellow. The crust of the earth it seemed was flaming and terrifying. The heat was so intense that all the oxygen of the air was burned up, and the legislators and all the people of the continent gagged and choked and eventually suffocated. The helicopters dropped like acorns from the sky. Ellen's hair burned back from the land, and from the corners of the state, and through the town, and to her house, and up the stairs and under the bedroom door, and though there was no one left to hear, just as the flames reached Ellen's head, she spoke out loud and clear. "Oh, you beasts, I could kill you all, for you have ruined my lovely, lovely hair."

PART I: HEADWATERS

THE BOY WITH THE LONELY VEST

Paul felt his mother's concern for him was sometimes love and sometimes merely hovering for she was always telling him to put on this or take off that, or add this or pull on that. He supposed she really cared about him, though once in a while he thought she only kept after him because Paul's father had died and she had no one else to care for. She always wanted him to wear a special vest which she said his father had always worn. It was a vest green on the outside and plaid on the inside, but she never let Paul wear the inside on the outside. "Plaid," she said, "was not for nice young men like Paul."

Paul did not really like to wear the vest. It cut him under his arms and pulled across his chest, but to please his mother he would always put it on, green side out, whenever she asked him to. He would lie in bed each morning before school and hope she wouldn't ask him to wear the vest. For the vest not only made him feel uncomfortable, it also made him feel lonely. Whenever he put it on, it seemed that the outside world drew back from him and almost looked the other way. He noticed that whenever he wore the vest even his good friends seemed to ignore him. He would be jostled and shoved out of the way at the drinking fountain, and no one talked to him. No one really cared about him. Whenever he wore the vest it seemed that he wandered in a world of his own.

One Tuesday Paul was lying in bed, hoping his mother wouldn't say to wear the best, but she did.

"Paul," she called from the kitchen, "would you please wear your green vest today? It would make me very happy."

He didn't answer at first. He thought maybe she would change her mind. He waited hoping. But she was his mother and he couldn't put her off. When she asked again, he said, yes, and he could tell from the way she was humming and half-singing in the kitchen that she was happy once again.

Paul, however, was not happy. It was as always. On the bus no one talked to him and he felt as barren and unhappy as the leafless trees that sped by the dirty bus window. And in the halls at school he was jostled at the drinking fountain, and his best friends walked by without saying hello. Paul felt very lonely indeed. He thought about taking his vest off, just to be free of it for a little while, but then he thought about how happy his mother was knowing that he would be wearing it. He decided he just couldn't let her down.

During English class a strange thing happened. Something so strange that it changed Paul's life forever. He was sitting in the back of the room. The teacher had moved his seat (because of the green vest, he was sure). Suddenly Paul's best friend Larry asked the teacher if he could borrow a pen. Paul thought that was funny because Larry always asked him for a pen. In his excitement Paul stood up and said, "I have a pen Larry can borrow." Paul reached into his pocket and pulled out a fountain pen that his mother had given him several months ago. When he yanked it out of his pocket the cap came off and the ink streamed down his vest. It turned the green material a sinister black color. Paul was very upset. Everyone laughed at him. Even Larry thought it was very funny. The teacher said, "Paul, you should be more careful. Now go and wipe off your green vest. Your mother is going to very angry with you. Very angry indeed."

In the Boy's Room Paul took some paper towels and blotted off the vest. It seemed that some of the green color came off onto the brown paper. Now everyone will laugh at me for sure, Paul thought. He felt more lonely, more afraid than ever before. He looked into the mirror and he thought. Suddenly an idea came to him. He could take the vest off and after it dried he could turn it inside out and then no one would know how stupid and sloppy he was. Everyone would think he just had a new plaid vest. He wiped the vest hard and stood in the sunlight near the window and the vest dried out very quickly. Then he took it off. He felt very comfortable. For a moment he thought it would be very nice not to put the vest back on. But he thought of his mother and knew she wanted him to wear it, so he turned it inside out and put it on again. He had an excuse now for wearing the plaid side out. His mother would understand.

Suddenly Paul felt very good, very good indeed, and when he came back out into the hall a girl passing stopped and said, "Why

Paul, how are you? I haven't seen you this morning at all. How are you doing?" Paul was stunned. The girl went on talking, "You look really nice, really great, in your plaid vest, Paul. Everyone will like it."

When Paul got back into the classroom, everyone turned to look, and Larry said, "Hey Paul, you look really great in your vest. Thanks for trying to loan me your pen." And the teacher said, "Paul, why don't you move your seat back down here. You don't belong away from people. You have a lot to contribute." And in the lunchroom everyone wanted to sit with Paul and listen to him and everyone went around saying what a great fellow Paul was in his plaid vest. At the end of the day the principal commended Paul over the public address system and said that all the students should strive to be like Paul because he was going places.

From then on whenever Paul's mother said, "Paul, would you please put on your vest." Paul always said, "Yes, I'd love to." And he would wear it green side out until he got to the bus and then he'd wear it plaid side out. Then everyone would be exceptionally nice to him. Everyone would listen to him and seek him out and respect him.

The years went by and in his plaid vest Paul was elected to all the highest school offices and made the best grades and went to the best college and landed the best job—selling bonds. In his first year and in his plaid vest, he sold more inflation-protected bonds than anyone else. It was not very long before the directors of the company began to notice Paul. When he wore his plaid vest, they went out of their way to talk to him and sought him out whenever there was a big project to be undertaken. Soon Paul became the Vice-President and then not long after the President of the company. Paul was very happy. But at the height of his happiness Paul's mother died. Paul was very sad for a long while, but his plaid vest pulled him through. In a year or so he was himself again and selling more bonds. And some of the biggest men from around the country came to him for advice, and everyone in the city noticed him in the street. There was talk for a while that Paul would run for political office and become powerful in the capital. Paul only laughed this off, for he had discovered something.

When he went on vacation (which was not very often) when he was alone in the mountains in his fishing cabin and it was late at night and he could almost hear the shadows from the moonlight moving in among the trees, then Paul got a certain longing he could not really understand. When this longing came over him, he would very slowly, almost sorrowfully, pick up his vest and turn the green side out and then put it on. All the old loneliness was there, the sense of being nobody and going nowhere and having no one to talk to and no one for whom he could care. And later, in pajamas, in bed Paul knew that his previous aching was caused only the vest and that the feeling was wrong and then he did not have to wear the green side out. But still he continued to wear it that way on vacations. It reminded him of his mother and made him think once in a while that he did not to run for public office, did not want to go higher in the world because deep down he was lonely and ignored. He had come from loneliness and ignorance and he could not escape it and did not want to.

Part I: Headwaters

THE PITCHER WHO NEVER THREW

Harvey Atkins lived in Sill, Nevada and played semi-professional baseball. He was careful and only played with teams having no more than nine players, eight of whom always had sore arms. Harvey was a pitcher—and no one knew how good a pitcher for all the games anyone could remember, Harvey had never pitched. Yet he had won by mid-season no less than twelve games. He did this in an interesting way. He refused to pitch. Each game Harvey would take his position on the mound and then say, "I don't feel like pitching today." The other players on the opposing team would come out from the dugout and plead with Harvey. "Come on, Harvey, you know everybody else on your team has sore arms. You know they can't pitch. You have to pitch Harvey. Come on. Be a sport."

"No," Harvey always replied, "I don't feel like pitching today."

"Aw come on, Harvey, if you don't pitch we'll have to call the game off and then the fans will be angry and throw bottles and everything."

It was true. The fans in Sill, Nevada were not exactly courteous. They had come to see a ball game. They had bought expensive tickets and now were sitting in the very sharp Nevada sunshine and waiting to see a good fast game. Harvey, of course, knew this. He was, in fact, counting on it.

"Nope," Harvey always said. "I know I just don't have it today."

"There's no way we can persuade you, Harvey?"

"Nope."

"O.K. we'll have to call the game off."

Then Harvey would make a suggestion. "Why don't we flip a coin or toss fingers to see who wins the game that we aren't going to play?"

The other team always said, "We did that before, Harvey. You always win."

"Well, come on. Give it a chance now," Harvey said. "Guess how many fingers I have behind my back."

The other team held a huddle and decided that since Harvey had won the last twelve times this way, their chances of winning would be pretty good. So they took a guess: "Three."

Harvey smiled and shook his head. He brought two fingers around in front of him. "I just won my thirteenth game," he said.

Harvey went on all season that way. Of course, the fans did not like it—did not like sitting in the sharp sunlight and not seeing game after game, but Harvey's record by late August was twenty-two wins and that was big news in the major leagues. The Sill fans liked the idea that their Harvey was big news in the major leagues. Sure enough, by early September several major league clubs had sent scouts down to watch Harvey. At first they were not impressed, but Harvey kept right on winning and a few of the scouts said among themselves, "Maybe Harvey has something here. Anyway, the boy probably deserves a break in the majors. In the big leagues one way or another we'll know in a week."

On October 1st the New York Yankees clinched the American League Pennant and sent for Harvey.

The manager of the Yankees said, "Harvey, we know this is your first trip in the big leagues, but we feel you really have something and we think you can deliver for us. We've decided to have you start the opening game. You go out there and win for us."

"You bet I will," said Harvey.

On the opening day of the World Series the Yankees took the field first and Harvey went up to the mound. He whirled his arm a bit and looked out across the tons of faces in the stadium. It was a vast blur creased only the aisles between the seats and the white hats of hot dog and beer vendors. The umpire said, "Play ball!"

Harvey walked down off the mound. "I don't feel like pitching today," Harvey said to the umpire.

"What?" the umpire said.

"I don't feel much like pitching today," Harvey repeated.

The umpire lifted his mask. "What's wrong? Your arm sore?"

"Oh no. I just don't feel I have it today. I don't feel like pitching."

PART I: HEADWATERS

"Well, I'll be," the umpire said and he motioned to the Yankee bull pen. The umpire signaled for a new pitcher, but all the Yankee pitchers got up and waved their sore, swollen arms at the umpire. "Seems you're the only pitcher, Harvey. You've got to pitch."

"Nope. Not today. Maybe tomorrow."

Now the New York fans were just as discourteous and demanding as the fans of Sill, Nevada, but they were distracted. For the most part they were busy drinking their beer and eating their hot dogs and they did not really notice what was going on. Then, of course, they saw the umpire wave to the Yankee bull pen and the bull pen wave back and that attracted their attention. Somebody said, "That punk kid is refusing to pitch."

"Throw that punk kid out. Throw that bum out of this park," a few other fans said.

"Yeah, throw that bum out," others joined in and soon there was a chant filling the stadium,

"Throw the bum out. Throw the bum out!"

Then beer cans started coming down from the balconies, from the boxes, down the aisles, rolling from the foul ball screens—at first hundreds of beer cans and then thousands. Thousands of beer cans and napkins and hot dogs practically darkening the sky. The grass of the infield was submerged in bottles and beer cans, napkins and hot dogs.

"We couldn't play now even if Harvey would pitch," the umpire said, folding his arms over his head and ducking the barrage.

"Why don't we flip a coin or toss fingers to see who wins the game we aren't going to play?" Harvey said quietly.

"I never heard of such a thing," the umpire replied.

"Why not?" said Harvey. "Especially since the field is too cluttered to play on anyway. It would take maybe five hours to get the field cleaned up. Go ahead. Get the manager and have him guess how many fingers I have behind my back."

The umpire sulked a bit. A bottle hit him and he dashed to the dugout of the opposing team. He came back with the opposing manager. The manager said, "Go ahead, Harvey, and hurry up. Put some fingers out behind your back. Hurry up! I'm getting hit out here."

"Go ahead, guess," said Harvey.

"Two," said the manager quickly.

Harvey brought one finger around from behind his back.

"Nice game, Harvey," the manager said, running back. "Nice game, Harvey. You had us all the way."

And so Harvey won the first game of the World Series for the Yankees. The fans did not like it at all and Harvey knew this and the Yankee manager knew this too. That night on the eleven o'clock news the Yankee manager announced that Harvey would pitch the second game of the World Series without the usual three days rest. That started the fans off again. They streamed out of apartment houses and subways and bars all over New York City and there was rioting—dangerous, sometimes deadly, and always frightening. The Commissioner of baseball decided that the atmosphere in in New York was not right for baseball, so he cancelled the World Series but made the Yankees champions because he said they had won the first game so easily, they would have won the others too. That suited Harvey fine. He told the Yankee manager as the flight back to Sill, Nevada was announced. "You know, I'm glad the Commissioner decided the way he did, because I really didn't want to pitch tomorrow anyway."

Part I: Headwaters

THE SURFER WHO RODE A LONG, LONG TIME

Otis McEachern lived just outside of Los Angeles. He worked nights in a gas station on a freeway near Santa Monica. Days he went to Malibu and surfed. Even late at night when all that could be heard at his gas station was the whoosh of passing traffic, Otis thought of nothing but surfing. He was twenty-six now and had spent all the time he could remember on a surfboard. His parents lived in Massachusetts. He seldom wrote them. They didn't approve of surfers. Otis didn't approve of people who didn't approve of surfers. Once, his boss had made some joking remark about growing up and leaving the waves to the younger boys, but Otis looked at him so hard and so fiercely that later in the day the boss tapped Otis on the shoulder and apologized.

Someday Otis knew the perfect wave would form up off the Pacific Coast. The weather would be right, and if he could catch that wave far enough out, he could ride a very long time. It seemed now that the biggest challenge of surfing was to ride for a very long time. When he had been younger Otis had thought the greatest thrills came from the big heavies which caused wipe-outs that left him hurtling thirty, sometimes forty feet into the froth. He had saved some money a few summers ago and on his vacation gone to the Banzai Pipeline. And it was great—the water picked him up like a hand and slammed him down like a sock, but when it was all over, Otis knew it wasn't enough. That's when he began thinking about riding for a very long time. He figured September would be the best time. The water would be warmed from the summer and the storms way out at sea might set up some big rollers. Big enough to be ridden for a long, long time.

The summer came and passed. Twice Otis turned down invitations to go to Oahu. "I'm not afraid of the heavies," he said to the other surfers who looked at him skeptically. "It's just that I'm beyond them. I'm onto something different. I can't talk about it. One of these days soon I'm going to get a long, long ride." The other surfers said that Otis was getting too old and they went off without him and came back with stories, which, though they interested Otis, did not excite him.

Then on September 20th Otis knew his time had come. All the night of the 19th he had stood beside his gas pump and watched the weird gray sky on the horizon as it churned and churned near the lip of the earth. "A good storm," Otis thought, "and way, way out. A good storm making a lot of good, long waves."

When six o'clock arrived Otis went straight home for his board. He put on the top of his wet suit and drove to the shore. It was still too early for the other surfers and so Otis started paddling out alone. The sky in the distance was still that wonderful churning gray. He was sure that if he got out far enough a big swell would give him a long, long ride. It was tough going getting across the breakers near the beach, but soon, when he had breasted them, he slumped on his board and began the easy natural paddle that kept the board lurching ahead. His arms didn't ache; they went by themselves and Otis, his chin resting on the top of the board, just stared and stared at the churning gray sky ahead.

He wasn't sure how long he paddled. The sun had not come fully up and he couldn't tell what time of day it was. He couldn't see the shore anymore, nor any other surfers. He stopped and put his head down. Water slopped over the edge of the board and swirled around his ear. As he rested he felt the board start to go up, and then after a moment of suspension start down again. "The waves are building," Otis thought. "It won't be long now." He got up on his knees, leaned back, turned the board, and waited.

The waves were bigger now than even he suspected. When he settled in the trough of one, it was almost as if he had dropped into the bottom of a palm which threatened to become a clenched fist. But Otis wasn't frightened. The swells weren't curling, and without a curl he could get a long ride. For a half an hour he bobbed from one trough to another, waiting. And then as he rode to the crest of one wave he looked over his shoulder and saw far away the silver caps that meant the really big ones had started to curl. "Just a few more minutes," Otis thought, "Just a few more minutes."

Part I: Headwaters

Two mildly curling swells hurled him up and then down, and with the backwash of the last one Otis knew the next one would be it. In the trough he lunged forward on the board, began paddling furiously. For the longest time it seemed the backwash of the first was still shoving him away from the distant shore, and then in an icy moment of exhilaration Otis felt the board start to rise. He got to his knees. The board wobbled. He got into a crouch ready to drop back down, ready to nose out if anything went wrong. But the board smoothed out. He started to soar. A quick glance back over his shoulder. It was perfect. He was just ahead of the curl—a curl that looked and sounded as if it must be forty feet high. But smooth.

Otis stood up, edged forward. He hung five easily, then backed off. "A wave this big and so easy to ride," he thought. He edged forward again and hung ten. He edged back, went into a crouch. The wave stretched forward of him, right to the edge of the earth, a vast forming gray tube—like no wave he had ever seen before. What would it be like in the curl? Could he get a long ride in the curl? He knew he had to try. He dipped the board, slowed. Forward spray stung into his shoulders. It was now or never. The spray hurt too much. He either had to go in or get out. He went in. The spray folded into a batter of water, tons of it hollowing over his body and swirling down of the other side of him. He was shooting forward on the floor of a conical cave of water. Water pounding into a roar that shut thought itself out. Otis crouched. How long could he ride in the curl? "How long?" Otis, excited, enraptured, shouted out, "How long?"

"Forever, man," a clear voice answered.

"How long?" Otis asked again, unsure, unbelieving.

"Forever man. Listen up, will ya! Forever and ever. Hanging ten—like to hang twenty?"

"Twenty?" Otis said.

"Yeah, man, twenty—toes and fingers, man, like this. See?"

"No. I don't see. Where are you?"

"Right on the nose of your board, man. Open your eyes, man."

Otis squinted. Yes, there he was. Right on the nose of Otis's board, a surfer perhaps only a few inches high, and he was bent over dragging toes and fingers in the curl. Otis shook his head. He dipped his board to wash the tip, but when it nosed off the slop the little surfer was still there.

"Say, man, you got a great sense of humor," the little surfer said, "but don't get too cute. You're in the curl you know."

"How long have I been in?"

"Your time or my time?" the surfer said.

"I don't know."

"What's a matter? No smarts? Your time, maybe two seconds. My time about three years."

"Three years," Otis said. What would it be like to ride the curl for three years?

"Like that, eh? Yeah, it's not bad, man. You get a good long ride and you can hang twenty whenever you feel like it, and no waiting around for the heavies to start. No missing the good days."

"How long have you been in here?"

"Your time or my time?"

"Oh, I see."

"No, man, I don't think you do. I dropped in for a while. I wanted a good ride and I'm getting it. What's all this talk about time. Incidentally you got maybe three more seconds in this curl—that's if you shift just right."

"Just three?" Otis said.

"Two and a half," the surfer answered.

Otis looked down at the surfer who was hanging twenty again.

"How do I get on your time?" Otis said. "How? Tell me."

"I don't feel like sharing."

"Tell me, please." Otis inched forward and bent down, the board started to wobble.

"Hey! Man, get a hold. Get a hold."

"Tell me!" Otis shouted. "I haven't got a second left."

"Hang five and wish," the little surfer said, "I'll get out of your way."

"I can't hang five in the curl," Otis said. "Nobody can."

"So don't. But you better get out of the curl then and right now."

"No. I'll try. I'll try." And Otis lunged forward and got five toes over the nose of the board and wished as hard as he had ever wished for anything in life. And suddenly he felt himself shrinking. He was getting smaller and smaller, and the little surfer on the nose of the board was getting bigger and bigger, growing up right past Otis.

"Oh man, you are the fool," the surfer said as he passed Otis. "Man, you are the fool. So long, man. I've been waiting for somebody like you for a couple of thousand years, man. My time or your time."

And then the surfer dipped the board out of the wave and Otis tumbled into the hollow for a long, long ride.

2

A Citation

ON SUMMER RESERVE DUTY you strive to be unseen. But on the second night of my final tour in 1973 a seaman apprentice named Hockmeyer, who sported a moon-shaped scar on his left cheek (an emblem of his proudly "totaled" Mustang), turned away from a card game in the Seamen's Quarters and asked, "Say, how old are you anyway?"

I thought about lying, then felt ashamed. "Twenty-eight."

"Twenty-eight!" Hockmeyer shouted, addressing the double bunks of the squadbay, "You're a fucking antique!"

No one laughed. Nothing funny about the truth.

"How come you're still a seaman? How come you never made a rate?" Hockmeyer insisted I become visible.

"I was never good at correspondence courses. Besides, I like to run a buffer."

"A real wit," Hockmeyer shrugged and returned to the card game. They were playing Hearts.

The next morning I stood in the head before the mirror, inspected the flab of my cheeks, the flesh handles around my waist, badges of married suburban life. Indeed, an antique. I was twenty-eight. They were eighteen—Hockmeyer probably seventeen. Inside the same obscene barracks language not a phrase of communication.

Part I: Headwaters

Had bones fused in my ears? My eyes gone experientially dull? I decided not to think about it.

Instead, I passed time congratulating myself that the last tour of twenty-seven-day reserve duty with the Coast Guard had turned out to be the plushest. Governor's Island, though only a nine minute ferry ride from grimy Manhattan was the garden spot of the Guard: District Headquarters, rural campus setting, lush lawns between the brick buildings, free gangway liberty (every night and every weekend) and meals to rival the restaurants in the city. On Fridays, for example, even lowly seamen received a mimeographed menu of seafood selections—lobsters, oysters, shrimp, scallops, and frogs' legs, which I brought home to my wife. The tour took on a dreamy sumptuousness.

The only complaint I might have made concerned dirt on the ferries that made the Manhattan/Governor's Island run; the oily scum on their decks and bulwarks could have been removed only by seamen and sogee powder. I was not looking to leave my assigned buffer. Moreover, one of the boats had a particular fascination I would not have wanted to disturb. That ferry was named for the Congressional Medal of Honor winner (during the Korean War) Lt. Matthew S. Graver. Graver's picture was on both decks, fore and after, a black-framed gray photograph and citation, vivid against the orange enamel of the interior bulwarks. I read the citation on each trip over and back. The initial few lines were straightforward enough. Graver had gone to the aid of a wounded buddy held captive in a North Korean cave. He burst into the cave, killed seven North Koreans, was killed himself. His buddy was able to escape and survive. Then the citation read: "It was found later that several of the enemy were strewn about the cave with their heads bashed in."

"Why is that sentence in there, Hockmeyer?"

"What sentence?" Hockmeyer was braced in the doorway and stared out, mesmerized by the New York skyline.

"The one about bashed-in heads."

"I dunno. Where you going tonight?"

A Citation

"Home." In the photograph Graver's head was about twice the size of my thumb. "Who do you suppose killed Graver?"

"A slope."

"Okay. Okay," I said, turning away from the citation. "Where you going tonight?"

"Man, I'm going uptown. I read somewhere there's all kind of free women at the Biltmore."

"You know where it is?"

"I'll find it, all right."

"I'm sure you will." I read the citation again. "Hockmeyer, you really think a North Korean killed Graver?"

"Who else?" he answered, doing an isometric exercise against the piping of the doorway.

"Well, I'll tell you, if you can believe an antique who still rides in a tandem and brings his wife ice from the river."

"Say, you're a real wit. A real wit," Hockmeyer said turning back toward Graver's picture.

"I'm thinking it was Graver's buddy. The one he saved killed him."

"Yeah, that's why they gave Graver a medal."

"Think about it."

"Yeah, I will, as soon as I get some."

I knew Hockmeyer would not think about Graver. That was enviable, for whatever else floor buffing led to, it was highly conducive to daydreaming. And reinforced by continual readings of Graver's citation, I began to fantasize the true situation in the cave. As the buffer moved in long vibrant sweeps across the classrooms I had been assigned to clean each day, my hands grasped a burp gun or maybe an M-14. I was Graver bursting into the cave, surprising the enemy Koreans, killing them, gunshots ricocheting from dark granite above and around my wounded buddy's cries. In the listing, rocking motion, shifting from one foot to another (which kept the buffer on its course) I was flailing a jammed rifle, scattering skull bits and brain matter around the moist darkness of the cave. That surely must have been the way those skulls got bashed in. The enveloping ferocity of close-quarter fighting must have accounted for it, and a rifle that didn't fire.

Why had an anonymous government scribe put the line in about bashed heads? Was it essential to say in 1951, our boy not only killed seven of your boys, but he managed to do it in a particularly authoritative manner: he split their brains. Was that detail only an embellishment dreamed up by a floor-buffer-turned-clerk in Washington at the time? It seemed to be a clue.

Maybe Graver was not a courageous, self-sacrificing hero. Could he have been a psychopath who had gotten the drop on the Koreans, wounded each of them, disarmed them, and then walked calmly among their writhing, defenseless bodies, smashing a skull here, a skull there until his saved buddy took him out of the action. That was a nice, safe fantasy for a reserve on free gangway liberty in the port of New York.

"That's a real screwball theory," Hockmeyer said.

"Think about it. Where you going tonight?"

"I hear there's a lot of free stuff in the village."

"Nothing at the Biltmore?"

"You have to wear a tie."

"I see."

Hockmeyer flicked a finger at the citation and said, "I wonder where Graver's buddy is now."

"Arrested for child molesting a month ago in Connecticut."

"Man, you are really sick." Hockmeyer said, disgusted.

"Would it make any difference? Wouldn't Graver still get the medal?" But Hockmeyer had walked forward to watch the docking.

On sultry afternoons I opened the windows of my four vacant classrooms and buffed easily to the sounds of the harbor. Seagull calls, sirens, horns, truck gears, and shouts, meshed in the magic droning. And when I tilted up the buffer, walking it along the baseboards, chalk dust and gum wrappers skittering out from the blurred bristles seemed as brain tissue scattered by a rifle stock or Graver's deft, vicious hands. That must have been the way it was. On fire to

A Citation

save a buddy Graver charged into a death rendered less immediately certain by the audacity of his plunge into the dark.

I buffed all morning. In the afternoons I arranged the desks in perfect symmetrical lines, notching each into the other with my eyes from four vantage angles. In the afternoon each classroom took forty minutes and then I waited for liberty.

"Would you have done it, Hockmeyer?"

"Look, man, I don't want to talk about him again. I get sick of it."

"Okay. Where you going tonight?"

"I'm going to check out Roseland. I hear there's—"

"Do you think it took courage?"

Hockmeyer shrugged and went forward.

Of course it took courage, not madness. Only the Reserve mentality doubted that. Still, why was the line about bashed-in heads there? A problem magnified, I was certain, by boredom and buffing. I read paperbacks. Hockmeyer stopped prowling New York. The card game expanded far into the night. I lay on the corner rack and listened to the seagulls and the horns. But at 4:00 a.m., for a hideous second, the clatter of the watchstanders getting dressed sounded like the muffled grappling of bayoneted bodies or rifle-struck brains.

"Where's a good place to go?" Hockmeyer said, "I mean you must still remember some places. You weren't always married."

"We like Radio City."

"Say, you're a real wit. I'm serious, man. I get shipped out on an icebreaker in three weeks. That's six months. You're supposed to be able to get it anywhere in New York City. I read that. Just tell me where."

"Hockmeyer, you're actually pleading. Has it come to this?

"Come on!"

"How should I know? I work in the city. I go home to Jersey. I never look up from my newspaper. I take pride in my buffing. I don't want to sogee. Shall I go on?"

"Fuck you."

The next morning there was an article in the Times on prostitution in the city. I tore it out, put it on Hockmeyer's rack. I dry mopped the classrooms, slept at the teacher's desk till coffee break, then finally started the careful buffing. The glowing scales didn't appear, so I pushed the desks to one side and spread a thin layer of white liquid wax. After noon chow, the old magic luster emerged, boiling out from the moving bristles. I drew creatures on the floor using the buffer like an extended finger. I saw Graver walking among those disarmed, prone Koreans, saw him kick an ear, stomp on a nose, bayonet each eye, bash-in heads. "Matt! For God's sake, Matt," cried his delivered buddy, "Stop!" But there's nothing to end medal-winning heroics but shots from a friendly pistol.

In the late afternoon my four rooms glistened. I crouched in the window ledge of the back room, sat watching the arbor, eyeing the Statue of Liberty. Graver was still a hero. Only the indolent cast derision on the anointed.

"Whelan's Drugs! I can't believe it. I can't believe it. I've been all over this city, paying out everything I make, and it's walking right in front of a damn drugstore. Just like at home." Hockmeyer was slapping at the clipping. "Take me to Whelan's Drugs."

"Which one?"

" 47th and 7th avenue. Right there, man, parading up and down. Move right in. Jesus!"

"It's near Roseland. You won't have any trouble finding it."

"I didn't go to Roseland. You have to wear a tie."

"You couldn't buy a fifty-cent tie? I don't think you really want to get laid."

"Oh, I do, man. I really, really do. In less than two weeks out onto that icebreaker. I can't figure out the subways. Besides, maybe you'd like to get a little. You just make an arrangement right there in front of the drugstore. I mean they're right there. All you do is walk up to them. Come on, take me up there."

"I'm not interested in getting laid. I'm happily married, remember? Especially not with some scuzzy seventeen year old drug addict."

"You think they're addicts?"

"Sure."

"Well, I don't care. I'm still going."

A Citation

"Good. Be sure and wear a tie."

"You're a real wit. Come on. Show me where it is. I'd get lost on the subway."

"That's harder than buying a tie?"

"Come on. I could die on that icebreaker. This is my last chance."

" Sounds more like your first."

"Fuck you!" Hockmeyer sulked off, didn't speak curing chow, didn't join the game of Hearts., At nine o'clock I let a lethal combination fuse: pity and boredom.

"All right, Hockmeyer, I'll take you up there and you can look around. It's a hot night."

"Don't do my any favors."

"Okay, forget it."

"Wait a minute. I'm ready. Come on. Come on!"

We looked at Graver's bulbous face, neckless and shoved down into the West Point collar. I thought, he didn't know what was in the cave. He just burst in. A hero. Not the look of a psychopath.

"I'm just going to drop you off, Hockmeyer. Then I'm going to a movie. You can tell me about it tomorrow."

"Right. Right. That's good. That's great. You're all right. I appreciate this."

"I'm sure."

"Look, how much does it cost?"

"I've never bought any in my life."

"How long do you get?"

"Why don't you ask her?"

"Okay. Okay, that's what I'll do. I'll ask her."

"Good."

At 14th street we changed over to the 7th avenue subway, got off at 49th street. Even from two blocks away the parade was obvious.

"You can see 'em all right," Hockmeyer shouted. In the block from 46th to 47th street, like a steady stream of lavishly dressed, signless pickets, they strolled back and forth before Whelan's. Smiling. Flouncing. Knit stockings, sequenced suit jackets, earrings, orange lipstick.

"Okay, Hockmeyer, you're on your own."

"Wait 'till I make connection, will ya?"

"Oh, for Chrissake."

"Come on! Just let me see how I do, eh? Wait right here."

He shoved me against the street post, bolted across 47th street and entered the line. He walked all the way to 46th street and turned back, all business. He caught up with a very young looking, plump black girl in flaming red, her lacquered purse swinging by her ankles. They stopped, talked. The girl turned on to 47th street at the corner. Hockmeyer leaped back across to me.

"America Hotel. Room #23. He pointed up 47th street. "If I'm not back in a half hour, come and get me."

"Look, I said I'd—"

"Come and get me. She's too much. Wish me luck!" He turned and ran down the street.

"Hockmeyer!" I shouted, but he didn't turn around.

I thought about going to a movie, but went instead into Whelan's. I ate a fudge sundae. I weighed myself. I stood watching my reflection from purple mirrors. I thumbed three magazines. I went back to my post on the corner. No Hockmeyer. In the thirty-fifth minute I started on 47th street toward the America Hotel, the night smelling like old tires left in the sun, though it was surprisingly dark. Nothing of 7th avenue's light streamed into 47th street. Suddenly I was scared. The hotel's green globe sign suggested an aquarium full, I was sure, of piranhas. I hated Hockmeyer.

The lobby carpet was a faded maroon color, dusty, worn to the webbing which scraped as I walked. The clerk didn't look up. He must have been used to lone men going in and out all night. There was a short, mammoth black man holding a corduroy jacket folded in his crossed arms, standing by the stairway. I nodded to him. He smiled, turned to watch me walk up. I thought about running, thought about going back. But it occurred to me that the fellow was probably a kind of reverse bouncer—a little impetus for those who suddenly lost their nerve. Trapped.

A Citation

Four unfrosted bulbs illuminated the orange, enameled hallway. I passed #17 and heard nothing. Not till #21 did the noise reach me, a thrashing sound, a muted cracking, a thud, then Hockmeyer's clear, sobbing cry: "Please. God God's sake please, please. Aaah!"

Elbows against the door, a bed turned over, furniture tumbling. Hockmeyer moaning, screaming, "Please. . .please, oh, please. . ." Then kicking. The squish of shoe into flesh sounding through the flimsy plywood door of #23. I stood, shifting from foot to foot, listening, "Aaah, please. . ..don't kick me. Please. . .." More kicking. There must have been five others in there. I looked down the hallway. The mammoth black man was standing now at the end, arms crossed, the brown corduroy coat glowing in the orange light. Hockmeyer had stopped moaning, but the kicking went on, crisp sounds like flailing a swab into a dusty corner. Then shuffling. I looked at the door handle, then back at the reverse bouncer. And I waited, waited and waited for total silence from the other side. I heard a door shut inside. I waited thirty seconds more, then I pushed on the door.

I expected the reverse bouncer to come bull charging down the hallway, but he turned around and went back downstairs. Something was blocking the door. I shoved harder, eased in. The shades were up. Neon red light filled the room. I stepped over a bureau, walked on a mirror, noticing for an instant my scared face, and then found Hockmeyer curled in a fetal position on the floor beside the upturned bed. His cheek was broken, streaming blood. Arms were folded back, palms gripping his kidneys. I took hold of his shoulder. He moaned, raised his head, "Oh. . ..oh. . . aah. . .Kick me to death. They were—"

"Don't talk. Don't talk, goddamn it. I'll get you out. I'll get you out."

He was positioned for an over-the-shoulders carry, if I could just raise him for a second. I knelt down, put one of his arms over the back of my neck. Started to rise. His head came across my shoulder. I pulled. He moaned. Blood, then vomit, streamed onto my back, a cold soaking. I dropped him, stood up, almost threw up myself.

"Kick me. . ..death. They. . .." He gagged.

"Shut up! Shut!" I shouted, shoving a towel from the basin beside the bed into his cheek. "Just shut up. Lemme get a hold of you."

I wrapped the towel around his head, knelt again and hoisted him up over my shoulder. His legs came off the floor. I wobbled out down the hallway, swaying, his right foot catching on the molding or rooms #19 and #17.

"Call an ambulance, " I said to the clerk, who looked up and shook his head.

"For Chrissake he's going to die. Call an ambulance."

The clerk shook his head. The folded corduroy coat stepped between us. I turned, went out down 47th street to 6th avenue, Hockmeyer colder and heavier on my shoulders. I walked out into the middle of the avenue and sat down. I pushed the towel against Hockmeyer's face. Traffic stopped.

The waiting room for the ferry, like that at the hospital, had mock leather chairs—strange, lumpy things with chrome armrests and gum stuck along the sides. I passed up three voyages over. I wanted it to get darker. When I finally boarded, I sat around the corner from Graver's picture, hoping that amid adulation and Congressional applause he would materialize and with the toughest bristles buff away my eyes.

3

The Revolutionaries

THERE WAS NOTHING MAGISTERIAL about her listening. He read slowly, awkwardly, pausing to guess out the translation, and whenever he glanced, however briefly, up at her, she looked supremely sympathetic. Her eyes, faintly moist, faintly puffy, behind heavy black-framed glasses, were full of solicitation. She had patience and, surprisingly, interest — as if he were not really the fifth backward Spanish student to enter the tiny chamber. At four o'clock on Tuesday and Thursday afternoons she dispensed "help" to those intent on passing. He figured he had a C for sure. He wanted her help in another way.

"This must really bore you. I haven't done my preparation."

She stood up, ducked her head—the ceiling rafter slanted—and edged around the desk. For a moment he thought she was going to attack him, and though he guessed he could fend her hefty weight off, the possibility unnerved him. She only went to the window.

"Look," she said staring out toward the library further down the hill. "They've given me this block of time. I'd just as soon have students here. They're liable to take away this time and make me teach another class. So you see—"

"I see. I just thought it might bug you."

She slump-laughed and turned around in the window, casting a thick shadow over him. She always wore beltless shifts, which, though they disguised the large waist he guessed was there, nonetheless made her already formidable appearance overwhelming. Large people, he was thankful, had gracious temperaments. She outweighed him by forty pounds, he guessed, but her face was full of kindness.

"If you want to go home—" he said.

"You're not getting off that easy," she smiled. "I've got nothing on all afternoon."

He expected her to chuck him under the chin and say, "Bear down, Buster."

"And just more studying on my own tonight," she continued.

"Oh," he answered and picked up the tiny reader.

She moved back to the desk, sat in the noisy swivel chair. "Come on," she chided.

". . . Only the . . . the dull—"

"Unattractive."

"Only the unattractive girls study. Conchita is . . . very—"

"More."

"Is more pretty."

"We'd say prettier."

"Conchita is prettier than Luisa, but Conchita is . . . dull?"

"Stupid."

"Conchita is prettier than Luisa but Conchita is stupid."

The next paragraph began with a phrase he couldn't unravel, so he said, in the firmest, sincerest tones he could summon: "Can you understand Cubans?"

She looked at him, smiled, "They drop syllables—a kind of Spanish short-hand. When I'm talking to them I get along pretty well, though I have to fill in a whole lot. But when they're by themselves I can scarcely pick up anything." She extended her arms along the desk, flesh jiggling.

He was careful of his entrée: "I've wanted to drive on down to Miami and talk with the Cubans, but I guess it will take a little more study."

"Ha! You can say that." Suddenly she turned red. "You're coming along all right, but I've had a lot more Spanish than most people, and I have trouble. Maybe next quarter," she added.

"Not likely," he answered. "I guess the Cubans have fit in pretty well over here."

"They're willing to work—unlike a lot of people in Miami."

"Yes." He looked back into the book. The phrase wasn't any clearer, so he decided to go further into the proposition. "Have you read any Neruda?"

"Poetry's not my strong suit," she answered, closing the book. "Now if he had put it into drama, then we might have gotten together."

"If I could get so I could just read Neruda. I think he's great, really great."

"I have the feeling his leanings make him—"

"Oh, there's no question about that. That's why she's so popular in South America. Don't you think so?"

"I'm strictly apolitical. Apolitical. We can call it quits for today. You've really got to do more work on your own."

He got up, took the maroon sweater from the window ledge. He pulled it on—feeling suddenly foolish, muffled for an instant in wool before her—struggling in the hairy dark. To cover, he said, "You're seeing my fraternity phase."

She frowned quizzically—watching his emerging head.

"Sweaters, pressed pants, sockless loafers, the whole course," he went on nervously. "I got over that a year ago." Everything, he suddenly noticed, led back to the proposition. "There are more important things."

"Like learning your verb changes," she added.

"Maybe," he answered quickly, "See you Tuesday."

"Not coming to class Monday?"

"Oh, then too. I really want to read Neruda."

Her laugh was a kind of sanction to leave. He felt he'd put the opening wedge in and he looked forward to the Tuesday session.

In class on Monday he noticed she was watching him; a puzzling interest he thought. This time he was impressed by her size twice:

when she came in with that galumphing gait as if moving in sections, and when, out of a sudden sense of inconvenience, she wrestled the standing lectern to a corner away from the board. My amazon interpreter, he thought. What an impressive addition she would make—if only he could convince her.

Tuesday's warm rain hardly damped his mood. He even did a little preparation. She wore a sparkling yellow dress and when she stood for a moment behind the desk (ducking her head) she looked like a brilliant shade drawn down to shut off the Florida sun.

"I brought a Neruda poem. I wanted to hear what it sounded like. I've read the translation."

"You want me to read it to you out loud!"

"Yes."

"After the next story."

"If you say so."

"He swiftly got dull Luisa dull Luisa back to school and her prettier sister several dates. Then he produced the Neruda poem. She sighed and took the sheet from him.

She scanned it first, then began to read the Spanish out loud. At first she was tentative, but with each line it seemed his confidence broadened. He was surprised to hear a touch of ham enter her voice. She got louder. Just when her intensity had reached a pitch to match her dress, she thrust the sheet back at him and said firmly, "That's drivel."

"Drivel?"

"All that business about United Fruit. Now come on, really!"

"You don't think it's true?"

"How would I know... Of course I don't think it's true. He wrote it, when? I bet sometime in the twenties."

"1927."

"See. I mean really, that kind of thing stopped a long time ago."

"I think it's still going on."

She looked at him quizzically. He locked his eyes on hers. She picked up the reader.

"Conchita's safer," she said with a curt, indulgent laugh.

After the session she walked down the metal fire escape with him.

"Can I buy you some coffee?" he said.

"I'll have some with you. Nobody buys me anything. It's unprofessional."

"That suits me," he answered quickly. "I've got two car payments to make this month."

She bought his coffee.

"Do you have a car?" he asked.

She sipped the coffee, put it down. "Always too hot," she said. "No."

"How do you get back and forth?"

"With these," she laughed, slapping her thighs. The sound was distinct, even above the clanking and conversation around them. He smiled. Suddenly she looked embarrassed, as if the blow on her legs had been too vigorous. "It's a short walk. I live on Anders."

"Oh," he said, looking away. "Where'd you get your Master's?"

"Indiana."

"Big school."

"A factory."

For some reason he felt himself turning red. The hollows of his arms felt very cold—and then he leaned in over coffee, the vapors almost beading on his neck. "Look," he said quietly, heat gushing up from the cup. "Look, you could help me out. You could be a big help."

"That's me all right," she smiled, picked up her cup.

"I don't think," he began again, but broke off, finally said, "Next Friday I want to go down to Miami to meet some Cubans who, who discuss politics, but I need someone to go, to come along and translate for me. I was wondering. I mean I know I shouldn't, but it's only an hour's drive and I'd buy your dinner somewhere if you'd do it."

"Politics?"

"You know, the exile and things."

"I don't know anything about it."

"Well, I know some things, and I could coach you."

"Say, how did you get into all this?"

39

"Into what?"

"All this political stuff. You don't look—"

"I know I don't look. Some of the guys at the house—we're going to pledge a Cuban. . ..Maybe. He talked to me about it."

"I told you sometimes I can't follow Cubans."

"Well, you sure can do a hell of a lot more than me."

"Don't swear."

"I'm sorry."

"I bet."

He smiled. "No, if it—"

"Please. I'm not mother yet."

"No," he said automatically with just the emphasis he needed—a summoning he was completely surprised to hear from himself. She blushed.

"I want some ice cream," he said, getting up.

"Bring me a cone."

"Vanilla?"

"Chocolate."

When he came back it seemed she had regained professional distance, all composure and dignity, licking her cone. He concentrated on his. Noise from elsewhere took over. He thought about apologizing. But the final crunch of her cone, she wiped her mouth and then said, "When do we go? When do you want me?"

He coughed, tried to cover his surprise. "Friday night."

"Where do I get dinner?"

"Anywhere you want," he laughed, forcing a certain green suavity.

"Don't say that."

"No. I—"

"Just not McDonalds. A cut above McDonalds. Understand?"

"Understood!"

II.

On Friday afternoon he vacuumed his Mustang, and with self-conscious thoughtfulness put the right-hand bucket seat as far back as it would go. He considered washing the car, but the day was hot. He put the volume of Neruda on the back seat. After he had picked her up and they had started down Rout One toward Miami, she reached around (the gabardine-like material of a new green shift scratching loudly on the plastic upholstery) and scooped up the book.

"I'm not expected to quote this, am I?"

"I don't think so."

"I suppose these people think Cervantes was a square."

"Probably." He down-shifted for a light.

"Well, the things I get myself into."

"If you're hungry we can stop somewhere along—"

"I can wait as long as you can."

He laughed. She thumbed the Neruda poetry.

"I can eat all the time," he said after some silence.

She read a poem out loud. "There's an image for you—a drying bloomer shedding one slow tear—Hehn!"

"Yeah. He really knows how to make you see."

"Hehn! One bloomer crying."

He turned on the radio. "You want to go along the beach?"

"Fine."

He turned off onto A1A. The traffic diminished and there were glimpses of the ocean, slate-grey, metallic-looking between the hedges of huge houses fronting the water. Further on, surprising clumps of pine trees shut off the view. She fiddled with the radio dial. He felt hungry, upset. He glanced over at her. It seemed her bulk slanted the car. Did she lift the wheels on his side off the ground? Not likely, but possible, he thought.

"I can't find anything." She turned the radio off, pulled her shift forward, slumped back in the seat. "I can't say this is the most exciting trip I've ever taken."

He nodded, began hoping for a restaurant.

"I make this run pretty frequently. We'll stop for dinner soon."

"I wouldn't be averse to it," she laughed.

At that moment, when the car seemed hollowest, a cement-tiered drive-in shop appeared. He swerved into Kelly's Snack 'n Snooze on (the sign said) "110 feet of golden beach front." They ordered fried chicken halves in the basket and thick shakes.

"Wanna go back there, on the beach?" he asked.

She had begun drinking her shake. "Suits me."

"We don't have to. I know some girls don't like to eat with the sand and all."

"Look, if you want to go outside that's fine. I'm not 'some girls.' Hehn! Besides, we would do well to avoid this scent." She tossed her head back and drew a whiff of noisy disapproval.

He chose the cement table nearest the water, about a hundred feet from the edge of the ocean. The table was circular and studded with dull triangles of tile, maroon, blue and green. Fortunately there was no breeze. He waited for the gnats but none came—almost, rather, a smoky, mucid warmth enveloping everything. The ocean lapped fraily, and far out its stillness became a dull chrome glare from the sun over their shoulders. There was a tanker on the horizon moving like a soundless model train.

"At Daytona," he said between licks of his fingers, "I used to drive down to the beach—when I was in high school. I used to drink a milk shake and watch the sunset. I couldn't afford the chicken."

"You were fortunate."

"Is it that bad?"

"It's fine. Just joking." She wiped her mouth. "A little old, maybe, but fine. Beats a T.V. dinner in any event."

"Is that what you eat?"

"Well, if you want the whole truth, I'm on a diet. A half a grapefruit and a T.V. dinner twice a day. Portions are small. Supposed to kill the appetite. You can have my French fries."

He pulled the basket over. "Sometimes I used to get out of the car," he said to cover as he scooped out her fries, "and walk down in the water. In the spring the temperature's just right."

"That's enough," she said, pulling the basket back. "Leave a few," she laughed. "Else I won't know whether to recommend the place."

He nodded, eating.

"Who'd you walk with?"

"Pardon?"

"Who'd you go down to the water with?"

"Oh. Most of the time alone."

"Come on."

"I had a girl for a while, when I was a junior."

"I bet."

He laughed nervously.

"You still think about high school?" she asked.

"No. Not a bit. I didn't know anything then. All the wrong things were important. It's embarrassing."

"Well, I don't know why. I liked high school. Everybody puts down their high school, but I think of it as a pretty good time. Pretty darn good time."

"Where?"

"Ohio. Silverton, Ohio. I played field hockey. Can you believe it? Now I have trouble getting upstairs." She pushed the basket away. It was empty. "Well? How about it?" she said triumphantly, turning on the concrete bench. "Well, are you coming?"

"Coming?"

"Down to the water." She kicked off her shoes.

He looked at his watch.

"The temperature's right, isn't it?" she asked standing up, then working her bare feet into the sand. "I mean it's the official way of greeting the sunset, isn't it?"

"We're already late."

"Big deal. Come on." She started for the water. He kicked off his loafers, rolled his trousers up, and still chewing on the upper thigh of the greasy chicken, followed her.

She struck a path, churning water out behind her ankles like tides around two piers.

"Slow down," he protested between bites on the chicken.

"Slow down, hehn! You catch up!"

"Now wait a minute," he said with more urgency than he contemplated.

She turned around, water almost to her knees.,

"I think we ought to leave. I don't want to miss the meeting."

"What goes on there, anyway?"

He finished the chicken thigh. "I suppose they talk about invading Cuba or running guns over there—"

"That's illegal."

"Revolution's always illegal."

"Well—all I need is to get picked up a bunch of anarchists."

"I don't think they're anarchists. They believe in government. They just want to get Castro out."

"I'm for that."

"We don't want to miss it. I mean the whole trip would be for nothing." He tossed the bone away.

"You threw away the best part."

"What?"

"The marrow. It's got the most vitamins. Believe me. I'm an expert at eating chicken marrow. When you live on T.V. dinners you end up eating everything but the tin." She laughed and tentatively kicked water at him.

"Are your feet cold?" he said, backing off.

"No. The only thing I worry about is stepping a chicken bone some litterbug has thrown away."

"He smiled. Water came over the roll of his trousers. His feet went deeper into the scratchy sand as the undercurrent passed back and forth. She seemed to be enjoying herself. He began to wonder if they would stand like herons through the night, in the shadow of Kelly's Snack 'n Snooze.

"Don't you think it's important?" he asked.

"What?"

"The revolutionaries."

"Of course! I suppose it's important. How do I know?"

"Well, I think we ought to get down there. The longer we wait here the less chance we have of helping."

"Look," she moved toward him. "I agreed to come along and translate because, because. Well, for a number of reasons. But I emphatically did not say I was going to help anyone. All I need is to end up helping a bunch of anarchists."

"They're not."

"Well, whatever they are. All I'm supposed to do is help you out. Isn't that right?" She stared at him. The tide seemed to get thicker. He released one foot from the suction of the sand.

"Sure. That's why I asked you."

"A favor to you," she interrupted. "To help you out so you can do whatever you want with them."

"I don't want to do anything special with—"

"But count me out on the action part. I'm strictly *apolitical. Apolitical,* and I obey the laws. I obey the laws and I never litter up the beach. And only once in a great while do I stand out in the cold with my feet underwater. Come on." She started back toward Kelly's. He sprinted up the beach and got to the bench first. Then, holding his feet up, knocked them together to get the sand off. He watched her galumphing toward him, massive and invulnerable.

III.

For a moment he thought they would be turned away at the door. He actually stepped back to check the tilted number on the faded white clapboard house. A face pressed against the screen from the inside kept repeating. "No party here. No party here."

He countered by repeating "Carolos Ariztobal. Carlos Ariztobal, my fraternity brother. My fraternity brother." There was, evidently enough, a party going on.

"Look," she said, "we've been around this neighborhood for forty-five minutes. There could be a party anywhere."

He said nothing to her—just continued to chant "Ariztobal" at the screen. Finally the door opened, held back disdainfully by a tall

Cuban immaculately dressed in a three-piece suit. She went in first, a massive blocker, he felt, if there should be trouble. A narrow, musty hall led to back room which was filled with people sitting on the floor. There was a keg of beer in the corner, a stack of unused cups on the windowsill above, but no one seemed to be drinking. The group on the floor passed a rudely-made cigarette around.

"They're turning on," he said proudly to her, pointing out a corner where they might slump down.

"What? What's going on here?"

"Grass. Weed. Can't you smell it?"

"Great," she answered sarcastically.

He slid into the circle so as to intercept the joint going around. When it came to him, he offered it back to her. She was still having trouble arranging her legs, rocking this and that to settle them under her. She shook her head. "That's all I need," she said.

He took three long drags on it himself, then passed it on. From across the room he saw a new cigarette being lit. Suddenly he felt her large hand on the back of his neck—like a liquid clasp of coldness, but sensual and attracting. He leaned back.

"What's going on here? I thought these people were political. I thought they were—"

"They are," he smiled, already feeling himself contract and float. "They are. We're just getting warmed up, that's all."

"Look, I came down here as a translator, as an interpreter—not an acid head."

"Nobody's dropping," he said with a certain sing-song coolness, feeling very good about his suavity.

"Oh boy," she said, slumping back, releasing her grip. Then she leaned forward again. "Look," she said, but he reached for the cigarette again. He held it back over his shoulder. She batted his hand away. He took two more drags and passed it on.

"Haven't you ever gotten stoned?" he said, conscious of a certain slowness of phrasing.

"Oh, I've tried it all right. The point is, I don't like it."

He stood up. "I'm sorry. I'll get you a beer. I'll be right back." He plunged across the circle.

There was a thin, red-headed fellow at the keg. He poured beers for both them, nodded. "You just come in?"

"Yeah. I'm looking for a fraternity brother of mine, Carlos Ariztobal."

"Cuban?"

"Sure."

"Well, there's an exile group upstairs. They don't like to mix."

"I can see that. This group doesn't seem too political."

"Bunch of heads. The room's right at the top of the stairs. There's only one room up there—kind of an attic." Then the red-haired fellow went out.

After he presented it to her, she looked at the beer disconsolately.

"Sit down," she said.

He leaned to intercept the cigarette again, took several drags and then yielded it up. "The exiles are upstairs."

"Sit down," she said.

"Okay," he said easily.

"Look," she went on, "this is not my idea of a good way to spend the evening."

"Is it too cold in here?" he said, conscious of a wide smile forming on his face.

"Very funny. I have a good job—one I need to get through grad school, you know?"

"Have some beer."

She took three long swallows. "Look, if I'm supposed to translate, that's fine. If I'm supposed to sit around and enjoy myself with people like this," she motioned toward the group, "then that's not so fine. Do you understand?"

"Of course, I understand," he said mimicking her inflections, then reaching for the cigarette again.

"Will you cut that out!"

He nodded while taking a deep inhalation.

She struggled to get to her feet. To keep her in place, he squatted down beside her.

"We'll go upstairs in a second. Just a second." He looked at her, seeing he thought, something beyond discomfort in her eyes—a back curtain of real uneasiness. He tried to think about that, but the phrase *just a second* turned over in his mind displacing everything. He suddenly realized he had no idea what *just a second* meant. None whatsoever. The phrase had become separated, a collection of strange sounds. That was funny and he began to snicker thinking about it.

"Are we going upstairs or not?" she said finishing her beer.

"Upstairs?"

"Oh boy!"

"Just a second. Don't you see that. . . I. . . I mean hear it? *Just a second*. Listen to that—JUST A SECOND. . . SEC. . . .OND. . . . SEC . . . OND. What the hell does that mean, SEC. . .OND?"

"Is there something wrong with you?" The tone washed him downhill for a moment.

"All right. All right!" he shouted standing up, losing his balance, shifting toward the wall, then righting himself. "All right! Let's go upstairs."

Before the ascent he did manage to draw her one more beer, though the plastic trapezoid controlling the spigot felt like a brick in his hand. The steps seemed interminable—narrow, scuffed, yellow-painted, sagging. They emerged right into the center of the room, obviously a converted attic. Their entrance caused a commotion. Two immaculately dressed Cubans sudden appeared beside them. They muttered. at him in Spanish. He sensed he had intruded but comprehended nothing. He turned to and she answered in Spanish quickly.

"What's the name of your fraternity brother?"

"Carlos. . . Carlos," he thought a minute. "Ariztobal. Ariztobal."

At the name the two Cubans receded into the group milling near the red-haired fellow.

"What did you tell them?" he asked.

"That we belonged here."

"What else?"

"That your friend invited us. Is he here?"

"No. I don't see him. What are they saying?" He pointed toward the group.

"They're not saying anything. They're listening."

"I didn't mean that," he explained easily, pushing at the bannister of the stairway. She drank more beer. "I meant," he went on, "I meant." He stopped, looked at her drinking, forgot what he meant and began laughing again. She swallowed quickly, watching him rock on the flimsy brass bannister.

"Stop that," she said. She pulled him away from the bannister and lurched toward the group around the red-haired fellow. Together, outside the group, they strained to listen, but the speaker's technique was low-keyed and rushed. Only phrases, words, filtered back: *Fanon, third world, health*. Then the noise stopped altogether and a small evidently nervous accomplice began a halting translation for the group.

"He's getting it all wrong," she said rather loudly. "He's mixing it all up."

"How can you tell?"

"Look, I know proper Spanish when I hear it."

"Right. Right you are there."

She grabbed him by the arm. "Say, are you trying—."

He reeled some under her grasp, but their eyes met—a visual collision he found lingering and somehow meaningful. She relaxed her grip.

"Why don't you do the translation? You do the translation!" he said, slowing, watching each phrase form in the air between them.

She flushed a full scarlet and let go of him entirely.

"You do the translation, and I'll get some more beer." He plunged into the group, elbowing his way toward the center. "I've got a translator, a professional!" he shouted. "She'll help you out. She's very good. I mean she's terrific. Isn't that right?" He turned back watching her, then reaching out for her hand as she ground her way through the fringes of the group.

Part I: Headwaters

The red-haired fellow said, "She know her stuff?"

"She teaches it."

"That's fine. Old Benny here barely gets through." Benny looked relieved.

It was a splendid arrangement, he thought. Things could not have worked out better. He pulled her into the center. "Just translate what he says. I'll get some more beer."

"All right," she answered, standing tall now, peering over her audience.

"She knows her stuff. Really knows her stuff!" he said, then forced his way back out of the group. As he started down the stairs, her voice, clear, increasingly confident settled across the room, initiating instruction.

Downstairs, he went back to the seated group, filled a gap and waited for the cigarette to come round. He closed his eyes, imagined her wrestling a lectern before the Cubans upstairs—whipping them into a revolutionary fervor with moist, compassionate glances and a torso stronger than any of theirs. She appeared to him in bandoleers, cartridge belts over the green shift. Even now, he thought, they would be loading mortars from his Mustang, aiming them at the established forces. Filling the charred night sky with bursts of gleaming blood.

He nodded, smiled at his own sensation, took the hot remnant of the cigarette from calloused hands beside him. It burned his lips but he managed two long pulls. He slumped back, fondled the white Styrofoam cup and then remembered his errand. He thought about getting up, imagined holding the plastic handle of the spigot but only succeeded in stretching out his legs. He lobbed his head from side to side. She would be wowing them upstairs, embellishing the red-haired fellow's speech, finding the right imaginative rhetorical devices to punch the message across. The word would get back to Carolos, back to the fraternity. Ate length he did struggle to his feet. He stood woozily at the beer keg. Then he became aware of noise—calculated stomping from upstairs.

At first he thought someone was demonstrating that dance he'd seen Spaniards perform on television, but the noise went on, got louder. Was she underscoring a point, emphasizing a tenet? Then shouting. Vicious shouting. The calling of a riot. A mass howling from upstairs. The cigarette stopped going around. Something was wrong all right. Beer spilled over his hand. The coolness spurred him to action. He stepped across bodies, hurried back up the stairs. The yelling got louder. There was a blue blur of bodies locked and shoving at each other across the entry to the attic. He pushed at them, but they were like a collar across the room. He tossed the beer behind him, then leaned his shoulder against the group. He edged in. The accusations grew more vehement. Suddenly bodies parted and he saw the red-haired fellow actually holding up his arms to fend off blows. His former interpreter seemed crumbled. Several Cubans were punching at them both.

"What's going on?" he shouted. Where was she? She had to be a head taller than any of them. If she couldn't be seen, it meant only one thing. She was on the floor. Imagine being kicked to death by Cubans, he thought. An elbow came into his back, splaying him out and forward into the worst area of discord. He grabbed hold of two necks, delighting momentarily in the ease with which he fingers dug in. "What's going on?" he shouted at the top of his voice, reeling and crunching into the center of the room. Fists streaked into his stomach. He was tossed in a delicious delirium toward the red-headed speaker, who grabbed him as if to strike.

"Man, like it's very funny and all that. Very funny. But who's the joke on now? Who, eh?"

"What do you mean?"

"I mean she's very funny and like that, and it's very funny and cool and all that, but look what's happening. For Chrissake, look what's happening. I mean bringing her in here was groovy and all that, but look what's happening!"

She was coming back into the group. She wasn't on the floor. She was safe after all. She was coming for him, he could feel it. Massive and invulnerable, she was wading through the crashing Cubans and would get him out.

"For Chrissake," the red-haired fellow said. "For Chrissake, she's coming back. Keep her quiet, eh? Just keep her bloody mouth shut. Benny!" He bent over the interpreter and caught a kick in the thigh. "Benny, tell them to stop."

She stood like a tower, flailing her elbows—clearing a path. "We better get out of here," she shouted.

"What's going on?" he said, dazed, fascinated, and delivered.

"Come on. Look, come on!" She yanked at his shoulder.

A chair was passed overhead. There came the splintering sound of a shattered window. Why bust the window, he thought? Why go out the window? Why not go down the stairs? The lights went out. Whistles sounded. For an instant he thought he heard barking. Then, his eyes adjusting, he saw only a blue, swirling, reflected light off the ceiling. She never relaxed her grip on his shoulder. More whistles sounded. Stomping on the stairs. He was shoved back toward the window, lost his balance. She snatched him up.

"The Pigs! The Pigs!" The red-headed fellow's voice filled the room.

A general scream. A couch turned over. He threw three punches into the dark, hitting flesh once—someone's back. Her hand slid down his shoulder, grabbing his arm, yanking at him. He tried to jerk away, but she pulled him to. They fell together. Her fingers around his wrist felt cold. Others fell on them. The lights came on.

The march to the police van was hangdog and embarrassing. He kept gyrating his jaw, trying to decide if it had become detached. She pulled at her shift—first hiking it, smoothing it, then forcing it down.

"This is kind of interesting," he said. "How do I get back for my car?"

She looked at him, with, he felt, infinite condescension. She tugged at her shift, stroked the side of her cheek.

"Hehn! Your car? My job?"

"Yeah," he answered apologetically

The first van filled with Cubans, then the second. For a third the police used a rented panel truck. They got in first.

The Revolutionaries

"This the white only truck?" the red-haired fellow shouted as he got in. "Racist pigs! Racist pigs!" A baton prodded him inside. The door slammed. There was no place to sit down. A sullen policeman in the front seat stared over a red flashlight beam aimed at them.

"She's too much! It's really cool and all," the red-headed fellow said sarcastically,

"I corrected your drivel," she answered, lurching toward the back doors. She pushed her hands into the ceiling to keep balance. "I listened to your drivel and I corrected it. This is a great country, so there. We came down here to translate. Nothing more." She grabbed him protectively. He worked his jaw incessantly. "But why translate drivel? This *is* a great country and they ought to know it. Your drivel, hehn!"

"Too much!" The red-headed fellow sat down on the ridged floor.

They leaned up against the back of the truck, against the locked doors. She still pushed on the overhead. He imitated her, straining as if it were a dreamy isometric exercise, watching the red flashlight beam as it lolled across them.

"We came down here to translate," she said quietly, as if tentatively stating what needed some confirmation.

"I brought you into this," he answered, pushing on the roof. "I brought you into this and I'm sorry."

"It was worth it," she said softly. "Not every day you get a chance to cut down drivel before it grows. Not every day."

"I wonder if I can get my car—"

"We'll get it, all right. Get back here and get the car too, you'll see."

"Too much!" came another exclamation from the floor.

"Don't pay attention to him," she said. "We'll get out all right."

He nodded and shoved his arms up harder into the roof. With a firm thrust against the truck's ceiling they rode steadily, in the moving red light of authority, toward liberation.

Part II

Mid-Stream

4

The Rescue

POLITICS AND POLITENESS, SOME link there, Hyatt thought. Index one thing for the State Department and spend the rest of your academic career as a good will ambassador.

The visiting Russian professor had been ushered in by the expected burly interpreter—almost Mongolian looking—and by a youngish State Department type wearing, Hyatt believed, an oldish Brooks Brothers suit: flared trousers, as if 1982 was not yet acceptable. Impolitely, Hyatt felt, the interpreter and the young aide had simply dumped the visiting professor off in his office and then retreated, as if delighted to be rid of the baggage.

"Ah, so nice to see you," Hyatt said broadly, standing up behind his desk.

The Russian smiled, offered a plump hand.

"I understand we have common interests," Hyatt went on.

"Yes—think we do have. Yes," the Russian answered slowly, carefully.

"I'll tell you what they are," Hyatt laughed. "No one comes off the academic path, not to this state—this sea of ignorance, unless he wants to see the Lindstrum files."

"Ah, yes," the Russian said, but there was some hesitancy. Hyatt suddenly felt that State had done it again: sent an expert on one subject to visit a professor proficient on another.

Part II: Mid-Stream

"The Twenties, that is your field?"

"Field?"

"Speciality. You know, life's work." Hyatt smiled.

"Life work. Yes! Life work."

Hyatt paused, assessed. "I simply meant, or better. . . I assumed you had come to Florida to examine the Lindstrum files as part of your research on the 1920s in America. Sometimes, of course, the State Department sends me someone whose field is China or Brazil, places I don't know anything about."

"Please—I apologize. I'm so sorry. Please talk slower."

"My turn to apologize. You. . . have. . .heard of. . .Carl Lindstrum? . . . Carl Lindstrum?"

"Labor, a labor—"

"Right! A labor leader," Hyatt fell into the standard pose of undergraduate lecturer. "Initial organizer of the I.W.W. Splendid speaker. Killed in Lansing at age thirty-seven, before he got off the ground, so to speak."

"Off the ground?"

"Established himself, made his way—succeeded."

Silence. Hyatt watched the Russian whose rimless glasses and baggy double-breasted suit conformed to the natural preconception-image of "visiting Russian history professor." The Russian stared, a strange stare—almost, Hyatt thought, impolite. Inexplicably the Russian was sweating. Hyatt scratched. Would the Russian ask about the files. Had he forgotten Lindstrum already?

Suddenly the Russian leaned over the desk, almost moving it with his thighs. "Extraordinary circumstances bring me here," he said hurriedly.

Ah, Hyatt thought, he *can* speak grammatically. He just needs time to rehearse.

"You don't need to tell me that," Hyatt said, laughing again. The Russian leaned back. "I understand all right. Nobody comes to this state, comes to this place, under ordinary circumstances. I knew you had to be interested in either the Palmeres of Brazil or Carl

Lindstrum. Well, nobody ever accused me of not doing my duty. I'll show you the files."

"Duty?"

"A manner of expression. You'll have trouble learning American slang."

"What is your duty? Duty what?"

"Duty to take you to lunch. How about that?"

"I must say, I thank you."

The Faculty Club was not crowded, a lacy, high-ceiling room, carpeted in worn maroon. Black leather chairs with inappropriate, Hyatt felt, chrome arm rests. Hyatt thought about saying the chairs must have been stolen off a Pullman car, but then "Pullman" would have to be explained and the remark would hardly have been worth the effort.

There was a silence in which Hyatt nodded to two sociologists eating in a corner. Between moist chomps on fresh fruit sections, the Russian said, "This Lindstrum important to you?"

"He's my ticket out of here."

"Leaving soon?"

Hyatt smiled, enjoyed the Russian's misinterpretation of the language. "Another slang expression. Lindstrum is the man who is going to get me off the ground. Remember? My book on him will make me *the* expert on Lindstrum."

"Oh."

"Once you're an expert on someone, you get job offers at other universities—better places. In short, you get out of here. Off the ground. He's my ticket back into—" Hyatt almost said 'the big leagues' but decided that would be a final straw, "back into higher universities, with more prestige. Did you say your field was the twenties?"

The Russian put his spoon down. "Ah yes! Labor, the twenties. The twenties and labor."

"Then you are here to see the files?"

"To see America and I must say, a lovely country. . . and the files. Of course, I am seeing the files."

"Well, that's one thing settled. The service is not very good here."

The Russian nodded uncomprehending.

"As a matter of fact I seldom eat here. Takes too long. Keeps me away from my work."

"I must say, I am enjoying it here."

"I suppose. But I wish they'd speed things up."

"I have three days."

"I meant the flunkies here."

"Flunkies?"

"The girl bringing our food. A student, I think, and very slow. I thought you were leaving Sunday."

"Yes. Sunday. I have three days."

"Well, two and a half, I suppose," Hyatt said. "You leave day after tomorrow morning." My God, Hyatt thought, he's got me fouling up the language. But the Russian did not call for an explanation of "day after tomorrow morning."

Finally the thin slabs of roast beef were served, and Hyatt and the Russian smiled at each other between long mastications. The sociologists left. Hyatt glanced at his watch. During dessert the Russian said, "Now I want to see the files."

"Are you sure you want to? I'm working on them this afternoon. I wouldn't be able to explain. I simply can't take the time off to give you a tour. But if you wanted to rummage through them—so long as you kept things in order—that would be all right with me. Do you really want to see them?"

"If Lindstrum important to you, then me also."

"I don't think that's the question. Lindstrum is important to history."

"I must say," the Russian stood rather abruptly up from the table, "that was a lovely dinner, worthy of thanking exceedingly."

Hyatt bunched his napkin. "Yes, I'm sure."

They walked back to the library, an imposing brick building with sealed picture windows.

"The files are in the annex area, in a separate air-conditioned room—but we have to go in through the main entrance."

"Outstanding grass!" The Russian motioned toward the central green of the campus, a lush area flanked by oak, mimosa and palm trees.

"One sacrifices relevance to beauty," Hyatt answered half chuckling.

"Pardon?"

"Another slang expression."

The file room, as always, was immaculate.

"This is my work desk. I'm up to 1923 on Lindstrum's correspondence. His general published papers—union exhortations, speeches, pamphlets—are catalogued in those nine cases."

"I'm sorry. I apologize. I'm so not good. Please talk slower."

There was real interest in the Russian's eyes, as if he were fearful of missing some aspect of Lindstrum's life.

"Of course, I keep forgetting. Is it easier for you to read than to listen to English?"

"I read very well."

"Okay. Okay." Hyatt went to the end of the room, reached up on the last cabinet. "Here's an index I did—published at government expense—on Lindstrum's papers. A chronology of his life, with the filing system call for each document."

"Government expense?"

"Yes. I got a grant."

"Okay. Okay," the Russian parroted.

"You can go through the index. I assume you know a good bit about his life. And then look up anything that interests you. You can work there. I'll be busy enough here." Hyatt tossed a folder of letters onto his desk.

"Okay. Excellent," the Russian said.

He sat at the desk Hyatt had pointed out. Ankles locked under the contour wooden chair, he began turning the pages of the index. Hyatt opened the folder, then brought his grey plastic box of oversize notecards out from the bottom drawer. The Russian bent over the index, running his stubby fingers down the page.

Part II: Mid-Stream

For almost two hours the Russian worked his way slowly through the index, pausing only to make notations on a yellow sheet of paper on the desk top. Hyatt was impressed. Head not five inches from the text, the Russian seemed totally absorbed in his work. Perhaps Hyatt thought, it would not be too inconvenient having him around. Serious scholars appreciated dedication, silence, and absorption. The Russian heightened Hyatt's concentration; his presence lifted the atmosphere of investigation to a competitive plane. Hyatt took off his coat. The Russian did not look up. Another hour and a half passed. Hyatt put some more yellow sheets on the Russian's desk. He nodded but again did not look up. Was it a phony performance—a pretended concentration, the way certain undergraduates pored over their blue books as examiners walked by them? At six o'clock Hyatt said, "Shall we have dinner?"

"So late, now?"

"Time flies, but the files will still be here."

"Excuse me. Please, but I would like to continue." He held up the last quarter of the index book. "I've this more to do."

"Not much of a vacation for you," Hyatt said, slipping on his coat. The Russian had turned back to the index. "Are you sure you won't have dinner?"

"Not tonight," he said, still turning pages. "Will you be back?"

"I work every night," Hyatt answered quickly, changing plans.

"Good. Good. There is for me not a great deal of time. Hardly."

"Okay. Okay," Hyatt said thinking, as he started for dinner, they do mean to take over the world.

After a deliberately leisurely meal at the Club Hyatt returned to find the Russian finished with the index and now with a stack of documents on his desk. He had dragged a chair near the side of the desk, and after skimming each paper he set them one on top of the other on the chair's green plastic cushion.

"Taking notes?" Hyatt said.

"Only few."

"Here, have some cards."

"Thank you."

"Finding what you want?"

"It will take time."

"Yes, indeed. This kind of research can't be done in a weekend."

The Russian looked up. Hyatt smiled, took off his coat, sat down to work. The room seemed to get colder, and the peculiar metallic scent of old filing cabinets and metal topped desks grew stronger. At ten thirty Hyatt put his coat back on.

As soon as his chair had filled up with documents the Russian returned them to the files. Then consulting his yellow sheet he drew out a fresh stack of Lindstrum papers. A regular beaver, Hyatt thought, he's planning to go through the entire file in two days. Impressive but not serious scholarship—a flamboyant pedantry, something for the teaching assistants to recount over coffee.

When at eleven forty-five the bell rang signaling the close of the library, Hyatt got quickly to his feet. He shove his swivel hair under the desk with clattering vigor. He turned toward the Russian, who was rubbing his eyes.

"Come on. Another day, another dollar."

"Pardon?"

"Slang expression. It's time to go home. The guest room is ready. This has been a good night's work."

When they had parked in Hyatt's carport, the Russian suddenly turned toward him.

"Extraordinary circumstances bring me here," he said.

"It's too late to talk about our countries," Hyatt smiled. "Besides, I know your interest in Lindstrum. That was evident enough. Come on."

But the Russian didn't move. In the yellow light of the anti-bug bulb above the kitchen door, he stared at Hyatt and then said loudly, "This Lindstrum important to you?"

"Yes."

"Most important?"

"I told you, he's my life's work."

"Life's work," the Russian repeated, copying Hyatt's inflection.

"Yes."

"Well, then I need another time—more time in the files."

"There's tomorrow," said Hyatt, shaking his head.

"Tomorrow, yes. Tomorrow. We talk tomorrow," the Russian answered, suddenly excited. "After more time with files. Tomorrow. Yes. Yes."

In the morning the Russian seemed even more frenzied. After a hurried breakfast he prodded Hyatt to get to the files as quickly as possible. And once there Hyatt listened to a continual clattering of opening and shutting drawers.

"I simply don't think you can master the files in two days," Hyatt finally said slumping back from his own cards.

"Only a little more," the Russian answered, "then we talk."

"You don't know much about Lindstrum, I suppose?" Before the Russian could answer Hyatt went on, "Of course, that's understandable. My book, I think, will put him on a par with Debs and Lewis in the public's mind. Right now I suspect only a handful of men in the world know his importance—another way, I suppose, of saying he's not important." Hyatt like the idea. The Russian was refiling reports. "You certainly are getting a lot of notes together."

"I need just some more in the files. Then we can have our conversation."

Hyatt thought, I can hardly wait. It would be like deflating an arrogant undergraduate—in a way a self-testing, for undergraduates were always miss-emphasizing aspects of Lindstrum's career. They continually needed redirection.

The Russian stopped searching for documents at eleven o'clock. Standing behind his desk he carefully went through his cards. Instant history, Hyatt thought, Russian style.

"You want to talk now?" Hyatt said.

The Russian turned, fairly beaming. "Yes. Now."

"Good. We'll take a break. I'll show you around the campus."

"We cannot talk here?"

"Oh, we can talk anywhere. That's why I thought we'd kill two birds with one stone."

"Pardon?"

"I thought you could show me your Lindstrum, while I show you my campus—though I hope it's not mine for long. Come on."

In the elevator Hyatt said, "Have you developed a thesis about Lindstrum?"

But the Russian, glancing at two undergraduates and the flowered librarian in the elevator with them, only smiled, then said, "Wait."

"Hoarding your ideas, eh? You didn't strike me as the competitive type. Afraid I'll steal them?"

"I do not understand."

"In America professors live in fear their ideas will be exploited by somebody else before they can publish them."

"In fear?"

"In a manner of speaking."

They went outside. "You've seen the green before. Let's go down by the pool. Now, what about Lindstrum?"

The Russian, still holding the notecards, cleared his throat. They walked beneath a mammoth spreading oak speared with strands of moss.

"Lindstrum was a man trying to get out," the Russian said. "What I do here. You listen? You listen?"

"Of course I'm listening. How do you like that tree? Who'd imagine a tree like that in this sandy soil?"

"What I'm trying to do. Extraordinary circumstances bring me here. You understand?"

"Of course."

"What I do is put. . . put my views in your terms, so that you, Professor Hyatt, can help me."

"Call me Ed. What about Lindstrum?"

"He was trying to leave what he knew. You see?"

"I don't know about that. The escapist view of political organizers, the frustrated man theory, has been done to death. Sometimes I think you Russians are twenty years behind the times."

"Not twenty. Sixty. Do you understand?"

"If you say so. If they ask me, I'll them you said it, not me."

"Tell them?"

"Yes, that interpreter," Hyatt laughed. I'll tell them you've been speaking subversion."

The Russian stopped. He turned the notes in his hands. "Lindstrum believed one thing all his youth. His upbringing so fixed—then when manhood, a new idea, to break away from his fixity. To help. To help. To make others learn him—the lesson. . . the lesson. He was good fortune."

"What do you mean his fixed upbringing? Lindstrum came from a fairly rigid middle class Norwegian immigrant family, that's true. But they were no doctrinaire Lutherans. Didn't you find those letters his father wrote him on that camping trip near St. Paul—a regular flirtation with Swedenborgianism. And the family library had 3,271 books. 3,271! I spent nine days going through that library. There was every viewpoint there from Marx to Kierkegaard, from Michelet to Spencer. I'd hardly call that rigid upbringing."

"But—"

"Don't bother to read me the letter. I know what you're going to offer as proof, the May 23rd letter—the May 23rd outcry. I have copies of it. But I'll tell you something. I have proof Lindstrum didn't write it. You get to know a man by reading his work. I mean the whole corpus. You see his style. You sense things, his reactions, even before he does. Do you see what I mean? Am I going too fast? But with Lindstrum, I know him. You sense things the way he does. So when something turns up that doesn't ring true—doesn't seem right—you know it immediately. Something in the May 23rd letter's phrasing didn't seem right to me. Probably nobody else in the world has read enough Lindstrum to see the difference. But I did. It set me thinking. I have proof now Carl didn't write that letter at all. His younger brother did. I have proof of that. Handwriting samples. Statements from an aunt. But even without that proof, why build a case on one letter? Besides, what was it? Only an adolescent outburst."

"Please. Please."

"Here's the pool. Universities in America have either sumptuous pools or sumptuous libraries Judge for yourself. It's three times

Olympic size. The library is adequate, maybe, for a small, agricultural Junior College."

"Lindstrum was good fortune."

"Is that why he was killed? Is luck something that lets a man get butchered with bullets at age thirty-seven?"

"He could break alone."

"I suppose we all break alone. Whoever heard of breaking together? Novel idea I suppose."

"You are not comprehending."

"Comprehending what?"

"Lindstrum spoke for freedom. Yes? Do you see I'm try to put my views in your terms?"

"Actually Lindstrum was more of an economic determinist than most American historians want to admit. In the '40's there was a revisionist clique which tried to see him as a libertarian champion—scholars affected by the war's pro-Russian sympathies. But it seems to me—and I think I speak with authority on the subject—that Lindstrum's values were cash oriented. He was perfectly willing to concede liberty for enhanced security. Perfectly willing to trade off minor freedoms for long range binders on management."

"My views on Lindstrum are this. He was good fortune to live in a land where change comes by wishes. Do you understand? I speak so poor."

Hyatt was watching the swimmers. He nodded.

"And Lindstrum was one way and then he moved. Came into another. The worker must have his freedom, he said. Freedom to move about. To make his living. To live his life."

"When did Lindstrum say that? That sounded like the so called Scranton Conference, but I don't recall that phrase."

The Russian shuffled through the cards, skimming each with his eyes, turning rejected cards under with, Hyatt thought, unbecoming anger. Perhaps one shouldn't shred even so weak a presentation, Hyatt reflected. One had an obligation of politeness for international reasons—even in the face of insulting scholarship. Change the subject, Hyatt thought.

Part II: Mid-Stream

The Russian started again. "Do you see Lindstrum was the man who was taking the risk. Trying to leave behind. Willing to. To go. To risk all. To put himself in the hands—"

"You think I look like a penguin?" Hyatt said, interrupting him.

"Pardon?"

"In the guide to freshman courses they referred to me as a 'tall penguin-shaped man'—the undergraduates I mean." Hyatt motioned toward the pool. "They put out a sort of secret guide to courses. They said I was tall and penguin-shaped, 'whose course is dull but dense, whose exams demand detailed comprehension—not for the timid student.'"

"I want to have Lindstrum's courage."

"Courage?"

"Yes. Yes. To extend. To break away."

"I've heard Lindstrum called a lot of things, but courageous was not one of them. Brilliant, dynamic, impetuous, a keen organizer. I suppose those things include courage. Courageous? Possibly. What's your proof?"

"It is. . . Read. You read it. Read it. You read it all. I can not say it well. But I say it here. You read it and help me here."

"Help you?"

"Yes. Helping. Helping. Extraordinary circumstances bring me here—"

"You've said that enough. It's hackneyed. Old hat. Trite. This business of help. I don't believe in cooperation between researchers. It's not scholarly. It's compromising."

"No compromising. None. None! No compromising. Yes! That is correct and good. No compromising. You read it. Then you help me. Read it all. No compromising."

Hyatt sighed. He took the notes from the Russian. He thumbed them. The script, though tiny and dense, was legible.

"You took notes in English?"

"For you."

"For me?"

"Yes."

"Why on earth take notes in English for me? On a man I'm an expert on?"

"You read. Then you help. You see."

"I'll read them tonight. You want to see anything else?"

"Read them now."

Hyatt looked at the Russian, then took hold of the lead colored fence about the pool. Staring away from the Russian he thought of saying: let's understand each other. This is America. Barked orders are very likely to get kicked down your throat—but would the Russian have comprehended? Hyatt decided the effort would not be worth it.

He said slowly, turning back, "I said I'd read them tonight and I will—while you're at the student meeting. Now let's get something to eat. Rest assured I'll read them—though, frankly, to be perfectly honest with you, they sound like the rehash of some ideas I rejected about Lindstrum two years ago. The man has become the handle for a lot of romantic dreams."

The Russian was looking directly into Hyatt's eyes. For a moment Hyatt thought the Russian would cry. Strange reaction indeed.

"You will read?" the Russian said.

"Look, I said I would."

"Thank you. Worthy. Worthy, I must say. I thank you, thank you."

"Okay. Okay. Now let's get something to eat."

During the meal Hyatt was disturbed by the Russian's unfailing beaming—rather, Hyatt thought, a madly idiotic glow, all out of proportional gratitude for simply considering his argument—even if Hyatt were, perhaps, the foremost expert on Lindstrum.

After depositing the Russian with the student group in the late afternoon, Hyatt went back to the files. He sat down, read two of the Russian's cards, then set them aside in order to finish some of his own research. At ten thirty he left the library and went home. He wanted to be in bed by the time the Russian came back from the discussion. Hyatt couldn't imagine sitting up the night trying to unhinge the Russian's obviously outmoded point of view on Lindstrum.

Not twenty minutes after Hyatt had turned off his light the Russian came noisily in through the garage, and in response to what seemed an almost desperate clattering Hyatt feigned sleep.

In the morning as soon as Hyatt heard the professor go down to the kitchen for coffee, he quickly got dressed and began bringing the Russians's luggage downstairs. Hyatt, awkward and overburdened had not quite reached the first landing when the Russian appeared anxiously at the bottom of the steps.

"What did you see?" the Russian asked.

"Pardon?"

"The notes. You read them?"

"Of course," Hyatt lied. He reached the front hall. "The argument I think is faulty."

"Faulty?"

"Yes. Exaggerated. You bend Lindstrum all out of shape, trying to make a libertarian out of him. You have to deny aspects of his thought."

"You won't help?"

"Of course I'll help. But you have a schedule to meet. I think things are better straightened out by correspondence."

"You won't help now?"

"How can I? You have a schedule. We can handle the inaccuracies by mail."

"Inaccuracies?"

"Look, I'm impressed with what you've done. It's wrongheaded, but impressive. Make no mistake about it, I couldn't equal it were I in your shoes. I can't read, much less speak or write, Russian. But you really haven't respected the files enough. You've been too cursory with them. I'll tell you something. In this country grants are hard to come by. I had to build those files from nothing, and out of my own pocket. It meant hunting up relatives and cajoling them, sometimes bribing them into giving me material. Maybe in your country all you have to do is submit an idea and the backing follows, but here you have to go on your own till you have a reputation. The files are huge, definitive. There's information there that simply can't be found elsewhere, information that can't be appreciated in one weekend. No matter how fast you work Now matter how quick you are. Do you understand what I'm saying?"

"We're going to the airport?"

"Of course. There's enough time."

"Then you won't help?"

"We've been through that. Let's go."

They said nothing during the drive, were mute carrying the bags in, but then on the resonant, freshly sealed terrazzo of the terminal, the Russian, seeing the interpreter and the State Department aide walking toward them, stopped, dropped his bag.

"I'm appeal you," he said quickly to Hyatt. "I'm appeal you for... for help."

"Help?"

""I'm stay to stay. Yes. Yes. Yes. Stay. Stay. Help!"

"Of course you'd like to stay. The files on Lindstrum are the best in the world. I put them together myself. I ought to know that. But you have your schedule."

"No. No! You comprehending wrong."

"Tell me what papers you want. I'll Xerox and send them. Now that's the very best I can do. My God! I'm not your graduate student, you know."

"Please," he looked frantically first toward the advancing interpreter and then back to Hyatt. "No. No. I'm to stay. I'm appeal you. I'm stay. Help!"

"Meaningful research," Hyatt sighed, "would take months. You have your schedule. That's all there is to it."

The Russian started to shake He glared at Hyatt, waved his hand and then shouted so loudly that Hyatt was sure porters outside the building must have turned around, "You... you... shit! You shit!"

"What?" Hyatt bellowed back.

The Russian turned and with the interpreter strode away quickly.

For a moment Hyatt doubted his ears. Then he exploded. He seized the State Department aide by the arm. "You let them be, do you hear? Did you? Well, I'll tell you something. Do you hear? And you carry it back to your superiors. You carry it back. And when you get some place at State—though you just look like another bureaucratic punk to me, a flunkie at Foggy Bottom. You heard him say that? Three days of expense and time and effort and work away from my work. For what? So I can be called a 'shit.' Three days of listening to arguments a freshman wouldn't have put forward. Three days for. . . for shit! You understand me? I intend to protest this right to the top. I intend to name you. You heard that? You and the whole damn State Department can go straight to hell. Straight to hell. Three days of international relations for that. He summed it up all right. Do you get me? Do you? Shit! Shit!"

Hyatt shoved at the aide, turned, walked, then half ran to his car. He sat knuckling the steering wheel, sat thrashing his left hand through his hair, and only the soaring throb of the jet's departure calmed his fury.

5

Accidents of Lust

Wide, immaculate blue water, shimmering and warm, almost hot, as Owen walked slowly into it. Embedded sand on each step of the white sparkling stairway at the shallow end of the pool. Reassurance against the bottom of his feet, eliminating skidding. Faint mist rising at the far end near the diving board. A sign posted near the outdoor shower contained a simple directive: "Never swim alone." Yet here he was at mid-stomach level, easing toward submersion in this widest, emptiest pool imaginable.

When the hot water reached his neck, Owen decided she had to have been going over 80 miles an hour. So fast that when he checked the rear view, she was not there—merely around the curve barreling after him. If his eyes had checked even a second longer he would have seen the glint, never tried the left hand turn, but it was just a darting check. Nothing coming around the curve from behind. Time to ease left before the on-coming station wagon. Easing left.

Submerging to eye level then totally in, just as the red Camaro careened wide as if to avoid his left front fender. But no. A crunch that tossed his van back, a crunch that knocked his eyes blurry, swilling/swirling in blueness. (The sky had never seemed so imaginatively blue.) Then a flashing, bathing whiteness. He was aware of his head throttled into the window, then whipped rightward—chest cushioning onto the steering wheel. The red Camaro thudded, plunged

Part II: Mid-Stream

more sharply to the left—seemed to pause (how could that be?) then sputtered, accelerating leftward across the traffic directly in front of the on-coming station wagon, over the curb and onto the wide lawn before the Y's parking lot. The red blur never got to the lot (empty of cars anyway) but stalled out in the thick mush now mud-spinning lawn. Owen's van came to a total halt, left wheel jammed in toward the engine, and the sky not so blue through the water as he rose up, letting the hotness drivel off.

The station wagon stopped and traffic behind it. Owen heard a woman suddenly standing beside his window shouting, "I saw the whole thing. She had to be doing a hundred. She crossed the double line. Right across the double line and nailed you. I saw it all. I'll testify. She could have killed us both."

Breaking back to the surface Owen wondered if he could float. The water was softly oily, not the supporting kind but worth a try. He spread his arms. Partially crooked his legs, gently pushing downward. The sky here was not so blue, softer, whiter blue and wisped with clouds. He wanted to be relaxed to relive what happened next in the accident. It was still the best part, the most vivid, the most delectable moment. The one that had kept him alert for more than a month now. It was the moment he saw every night before he dropped off to sleep, and it was the moment he gathered back up lovingly every morning.

Owen opened his car door. The woman stood back. "Believe me I'll testify. You can have my name and number. She ought to lose her license." But Own wasn't listening yet. He was drawn to the red Camaro inert in the soggy lawn, for he must have seen. The insistent woman said, "I have a pen. You have a piece of paper?" Still staring at the inert red Camaro, Owen said, "Piece of paper?"

"I'll give you my phone number. People like her should be off the road. Never allowed on it. She's a killer."

"Killer?" Own said.

"You know what I mean. You got some paper? Never mind. Here's a pad on your dash."

"Dash?"

It was hard to float all right. Maybe the water's too warm. I'm too heavy. Owen worked his arms in slow flutter, contemplated the off-white blue of the Florida sky, saw two crows flying surprisingly high, then settling in on the high cabbage palms outside of the pool.

Owen stepped away from the van, moved toward the mud trapped Camaro.

"Look," the woman shouted after him, "I'm putting the pad back with my name and number. I'm putting it back in your car. I'll testify. You listening?"

"Yes," Owen answered. He stared through the window of the Camaro. A young blonde woman in jeans, with a tank top that ended just below her breasts. Owen stared at her stomach golden silky downed and gleaming in the sunlight. The window came down. The warm electronic sound unzipped his soul.

"You all right? " Owen said.

"No," came a quick answer. "Can you shut that stupid bitch up?"

"You hurt?" Owen said.

"How the fuck should I know? Can't you shut her up? The bitch will testify, will testify. We've got that."

Early that morning his mother said from her wheelchair. "You're not supposed to swim alone. You have a heart attack and no one's there to bring you up. They're liable. They don't want to be liable."

No one's here by the pool, but he thought—no heart attack today.

"Before you take your dip," his mother had said (was there a mild sarcasm to the word dip?) "fix me a drink. Or better yet, just add ice to the one's that's in the refrigerator and maybe another olive."

"Olives and spice drops," Owen said.

"What?" his mother said.

"Olive or spice drop?" Owen answered going into the narrow galley kitchen that was also a walkway to the living and the three small bedrooms of her 'life-care' condominium.

"What?" she asked again.

So he was beyond hearing aid range.

"It's not important," Owen shouted.

But of course the silken blond, suffused and gleaming stomach was important, supremely important. She had a small silver steel ring piercing through a flap of her navel. The ring caught the sunlight dappling his eyes for an instant. Then she was out of the car.

"You're okay, then?" Owen asked.

But she was not interested in his question. She pointed over his shoulder at the station wagon woman. "Why don't you go along home? Just drive off. You've done your fucking civic duty. Now get out of here. You'll get your chance to testify."

Owen imagined he could get both hands around that incredibly svelte, soft stomach. He could lick around that dazzling ring, but abruptly even before he could drop to his knees and grab that golden flesh to his mouth, she swiveled back into the car and slumped over the wheel, then pulled the door closed. Part of the nape of her neck between the lush blond strands was visible as she pushed her face into the wheel.

"Are you okay?" Owen asked hotly against the doorframe.

"No," she murmured. Her back also had the same almost iridescent blond fuzz, like a moist frosting on a slice of perfectly blended sponge cake, to be slowly devoured, slowly pulled over his head, slowly burrowed in.

When the first fire-truck got there, they put her on a stretcher right beside Owen; he could only stare at that perfect stretch of stomach on the ground, before they picked the stretcher up. As they started to move her, Owen shouted. "Your name? Your name? How do I reach you? Is it your car?"

"Deirdre.. Deirdre Mountis."

"*Mountis* turned over in Owen's mind. "And the car?"

"My boyfriend's. Earl's fully covered."

Fully covered. Fully covering her. Surely she wouldn't but could he share that glistening golden fleece—the cashmere immaculate glove turned inside out to receive him.

"I'm fully covered too," Owen said.

"So we're all covered," the EMS said.

"Here's my card. My card, Deidre." Owen tried to press the card onto that incredible stomach, but despite the straps she managed to ease her right hand across the pelt, stifling him. She turned her palm up and he put his business card into it.

"I can't read it. Who was that fucking bitch?"

"Her name's in my van," Owen apologized. "I'm Owen Metcalf. I work at Sharfman's. I'm a manager. I have full coverage through the business. There shouldn't be any trouble."

"Tell that to Earl," she said. "Wait till Earl sees his car."

"I can take care of Earl," Owen quickly said.

She laughed in an irritating way.

Owen said, "I meant I could cover his expenses."

"You'd do that? It wasn't your fault you know."

"I would if you wanted me to." Owen said, wondering why. "What does fault mean?"

"Take it up later," the EMS said raising the stretcher to belt level.

That golden stomach suddenly rushed upwards toward Owen's chest. Glistening and downy soft and plunging right toward his face. All that svelte smelling ovular smoothness sponginess folded around his cheeks. So knead-able, so engulfing.

He sprinted toward the far end of the pool thrashing furiously to dissipate an aching longing flooding into his torso. He did an open turn against the pool's far wall, kicked away, clawing through the unbuckling water, gloriously draining his lust. Shoulders working till they burned, legs flailing a delicious froth.

II.

Entry to the dining hall of the life care residence was always an embarrassing moment, as if Owen had to relive the tough negotiation that had gotten, over strong objections, his mother in a wheel chair being admitted. The dining hall had rose carpeting, thick pile so tightly packed as to present no difficulty for his mother's wheel chair, clicking along as they entered. It was the sort of entrance he knew she savored.

It had been his lengthy negotiation with the management that had gotten wheel chairs into the dining room in the first place. But all that work counted for nothing. Entrance was all. The original contract had forbidden such mobility aids. You had to be ambulatory to use the mammoth dining facilities and of course enjoy the mutual viewing. In a way the wheel chair had moved things along. His mother's infinitely deliberate slow walk with her aluminum walker had caused far more comment and disruption. Maybe the management had thought about that. She liked to wave to people she knew or didn't know for that matter. She wanted to be presented each afternoon at 5:05 p.m. to the adoring multitude who, if they were not adoring she preferred not to know. Since her hearing had disintegrated it had been harder and harder to find someone willing to eat with her. When he was not irritated by her constant and unanswerable "What? What?" he imagined it was no joy to be in her soundless world—moving, soundless creatures. It was the thunking crunch of the lambasted front fender that triggered his receptivity to that golden shimmering stomach, that taut, rippleless flesh— like warm water. He was sure of it. It had all he could do not to drop on his knees before Deirdre's strapped form on that fireman-carried litter.

The question, once the transfer to her dining chair had been accomplished and the folded wheelchair put against the wall, was always the same. "Do you remember what we ordered?"

Owen shook his head. He wanted to say. I wasn't here when you ordered the meal a month ago, but did not, lest he have to deal with the terrifying loud, "What? What?" It was policy to submit a meal order on a long mimeographed sheet 3 to 4 weeks beforehand.

" I always mean to get a copy, but I keep forgetting to tell Dottie to do it," his mother said. "And she keeps forgetting to remind me. Of course, forgetting is just part of it," she said smiling. "I think I've told you about the forgetting."

"Yes," Owen answered, nodding exaggeratedly to cut off the inevitable "What? What?"

"I've probably told you that I should say the change from 65 to 75 is the most dramatic. That's a real difference. 55 to 65 isn't much, but 65 to 75 is really dramatic."

Not a lot of drama, Owen thought, in her soundless world.

Then came the second expected series of declarations: "You'll notice Barrett never acknowledges me in here." Her eyes flicked around the large room, over its sculpted ceiling painted a light maroon. "At first I thought it was deliberate slight, as if he didn't want to be associated with me in public, but lately I see the wisdom in it."

"The place is full of gossips," Owen completed her sentence.

"What? What?" she leaned across the table.

"Nothing. Nothing," Owen shook his head.

"Barrett doesn't want the old biddies to gossip. He's very wise, though sometimes I think he goes too far with that denial. But he's about the most eligible bachelor here. He loved his Mary, just as I loved your father. We're both just waiting for reunion with them."

"After death?" Owen asked.

"What? What?"

"After you've died," Owen said more loudly, mouthing the words.

"I haven't died yet," she smiled. "Might seem that way, but not yet. Not Barrett either."

Owen nodded signaling comprehension.

"Barrett always sits in that far corner to your right in the back. You can go ahead and look. He won't acknowledge you. Sometimes he sits with his market buddies but often he eats alone. I don't like to eat alone."

"I sensed that," Owen said.

"What? What?"

"Nothing!" Owen shouted. A few people looked over. His mother waved to them.

"That's Vanessa Silver. She thinks she owns Barrett. But she doesn't. Barrett comes over every night to tuck me in. We have a night cap and watch Wheel of Fortune."

Owen smiled approval, giving up the possibility of conversation.

Part II: Mid-Stream

The meal turned out to be beef brisket on soggy toast points with green beans and orange jello salad. There was endless iced tea.

Back in the apartment, after he had gotten his mother another drink of bourbon and two cubes of ice, Owen put in a call to the Mountis household. After some negotiations Deidre came on the line.

"I'm in Florida, visiting my mother, but I wanted to find out if you were okay," Owen said.

"Who is this?"

"Owen Metcalf, the fellow in the van, in your accident. You know outside the Y three Sundays ago, in the morning."

"Oh, yeah. I'm okay. Oh, sometimes a pain in my neck, but–"

"Is your stomach okay?"

"Of course. Why 'dya ask that?"

Owen scrambled, paused, then rushed into it: "Sometimes accidents affect how you digest things; trauma can upset the way things are absorbed into your digestive system. Can upset the smooth functioning, the supple absorption of nutrients-—"

"Look, don't call me up with that crap. Just don't call. Jesus!" and she hung up.

"Can you get me my hand mirror on my bureau, Owen? Barrett's coming over for Wheel of Fortune, and I want to put on some lipstick."

Still reeling from Deirdre's rejection, Owen, obediently, fetched the mirror and handed it to his mother. She set her cigarette down and began applying lipstick, pausing to pick up the mirror and check her handiwork.

"Is it a date?" Owen asked.

"A date? Do we have those at our age?" his mother answered. "I suppose you could call it a date—an inside date."

"He doesn't mind your smoking?"

"Barrett's a cigar smoker himself. And that has its plus side. Your father never smoked. Never understood my needs that way."

"But he certainly accommodated them."

His mother looked at him measuring the resentment, apparently thinking about it. "He did say his clothes smelled of cigarette smoke. I suppose you think the same thing."

"I do bring the scent back to New Jersey in my baggage." Owen said, and almost instantly regretted.

"You have very little to put up with in your life. An extra laundering, is that insuperable?"

"Of course not," Owen answered.

"So let's not talk about it, shall we? Let's not spoil Barrett's visit."

Chastised Owen set about wiping the galley kitchen counter when Barrett came in. He was a much shorter man than Owen's father, much thinner, fitter, and in a brown suit with a black tie. He had a thinning mustache, and perhaps he walked with a very slight limp, Owen couldn't quite decide. He had asked Barrett about it, after Owen's father's funeral, but the slender man denied any problem. Instead he offered the observation that alone among men his age he had a very flat stomach, and in fact wore the same size suit he had worn at age twenty-five. It seemed Barrett mistook concern for criticism.

"How's my Evy tonight?" Barrett said, leaning down to kiss Owen's mother.

"Oh, Barrett—the same as every night."

"You look more radiant now that you son's here to cheer you up."

"Oh, Barrett, come on. Owen comes often enough."

"More than my daughter, that's for sure."

"Owen, fix Barrett his drink, will you? You know the routine."

Owen brought Barrett his bourbon neat in an old fashion glass. Barrett had settled into the yellow heavily padded chair Owen's father used every night to watch Wheel of Fortune—a routine Owen found peculiarly vile.

"Turn the sound up." His mother said.

Barrett took out a cigar and Owen left them vaguely rocking in their yellow chairs as Vanna began turning squares over. He retreated to his mother's bedroom, sat for a moment at his father's leather-topped desk. He wondered where the short brass lamp with its marble square base had gone to. Sold off after his father's death, since she couldn't use the desk anyway? Otherwise the desk seemed still to hold all the artifacts that suggested his father might return in the morning. A walnut tray for fresh mail (with brass clamp gripping unopened bills) a leather box for his pocket watch, a pewter business card holder empty and cool to the touch. A calculator with its numerical display tilted up from the buttons and with nifty green illumination. His father loved precise calculations and prized the legibility of the display.

Owen left the desk and flopped down on his father's side of the king size bed. He was asleep when the clicking of his mother's wheelchair coming into the room startled him.

Barrett was pushing the chair.

"Tired from the flight?" Barrett said.

"I guess so."

Barrett wheeled his mother over to the entrance to her bathroom and then said, "Goodnight Evy, I'll let myself out. See you tomorrow."

"Thanks so much for coming over. Owen will carry out the duties now." She waved to Barrett who seemed to quicken his step down the hallway to the front door. Then she swivelled toward Owen. "Now you'll have to do the Anise role–and I'm sorry for that. Under the arms please."

Owen eased her out of the chair by grasping her arm pits and then walk-waddled her toward the toilet. "I can take it from here. Just close the door and let me work." His mother said.

Afterwards, when he had gotten his mother into the bed and adjusted her covers, Owen said, "Did I deprive you of Barrett's tucking you in? I could have gone to the other room. I don't want to disturb your normal routine."

"Not to worry," his mother answered. "The routine is comforting and all, but truth to tell he has very grabby hands, if you know what I mean."

"Grabby hands?"

"All over my breasts."

"Please."

"You're such a prude," his mother said.
"I suppose." Owen answered.

III.

Owen slept in Anise's room. She was the young Jamaican woman he had hired to be the live-in attendant to his mother. Whenever Owen visited she was delighted to spend time with her relatives in Miami. Her room was between the study/t.v. room and the master bedroom. The room was painted yellow and had twin beds with yellow striped bedspreads. Owen imagined he slept in the bed Anise didn't use, but the beds were identical and he couldn't be sure. There were Victoria's Secret catalogs on the night stand between the beds. Owen hoped Deirdre ordered identical gear, nifty intoxicating blue or black sheer patches with string ties around silken thighs, buttocks, breasts. He poured over the catalogs using the night stand light that he realized had been on his father's desk. He imagined his father pouring over calculations and tax options under the lamp, while Owen contemplated Deirdre decked out in sheer something shielding only the sought-after finale of that incredible golden fleeced stomach with its beguilingly smooth, lickable, gentle hillocks of flesh. The Camaro slammed into his van transporting him magically into a frenzy of grabby hands, and breath-stopping lurches. At least he knew she was not hospitalized—perfectly sound, perfectly sleek but, alas, not at all receptive to his phone entreaties. He'd set back his cause with such solicitations. She was immune to conventional wooing, or so it seemed. Maybe Earl had gotten her with his car. Maybe she was a sucker for a red Camaro. When he went back home, he'd buy a flashier car, was that it?

The morning was moist, cool, but the pool water was again near hot. Again he was alone, violating the life-care rules. This time he was able to float a bit. A gentle circular movement of his arms, a gentle downthrust of his legs clamped together, buoyed him up for a few seconds, until the exercise could be repeated. He watched the circling crows and the hazy sunshine backlighting the cabbage palms. It was the remembered muffled crunch of the front fender collapsing that triggered intense interest in her midriff. Despoilation of fit and finish sent him weakly celebrating her stunning pelt. How could that be? Accidental collision freed up a torrent of sentiment, an explosive longing. The near death shock opening the life force—was that it? Too ridiculous, but there she was skittering across the water's surface, resting sublimely on an overinflated white water mattress. Owen thought, as he side stroked through the hot water, ah, mount the Mountis.. Grabby hands, indeed.

For breakfast in the apartment they had a basket of bran muffins, coffee, and Bloody Marys. He spent the rest of the morning going through his father's desk, dispensing with bills, and filing documents. He discovered a Sears Roebuck life insurance policy that paid two thousand dollars for an accidental death. His father had never mentioned it. His mother seemed pleased they could file for the money. His father had died after falling in the bedroom and hitting his head on a sharp object. He had assumed the accident occurred in the bathroom, but his mother insisted his unsteady father never got that far. In the middle of the night he fell against the edge of her French Provincial tall lingerie chest of drawers backed against the wall next to the bathroom door. Often enough Owen had considered the rounded edges of the chest's top a danger in the small bedroom. Since his father had a terminal blood disease, his mother referred to the accident as "a blessing." And so indeed it seemed since his father had lived almost 18 months on transfusions as his immune system disintegrated.

"What's better than found money like that?" Barrett said enthusiastically as they settled in to watch Jeopardy, that night. "And from Sears Roebuck! That's real justice."

"You're in good hands," Owen offered and watched Barrett laugh.

"Two grand will buy a lot of bourbon, Evy." Barrett said, but Owen found the expression startlingly tasteless. He looked at his mother who only blankly sipped her vodka.

When Owen wheeled her to the bedroom after the show and then helped her into the bathroom, he stood for a while looking at the edge of the lingerie chest. He expected to see some sort of indentation, some chip or stain, some trace of the back of his father's skull. But the edge seemed flawless–gold gilding intact, paint whole and appropriately antiqued.

"You'd never know Dad killed himself on this chest," he said to his mother, helping her back into her wheel chair.

"Really?" She answered.

"Not a mark."

"Anise cleaned everything up–she likes to keep everything immaculate. Besides, we won't have to prove the accident occurred will we?"

"The death certificate says accident—that's all we'll need." Owen said.

"I don't like talking about it."

"Okay. Let's not. Instead, I'll talk about my accident."

"What?"

"Yeah, I had one at home, in front of the Y. A young woman in a red Camaro hit me, did about two thousand dollars' worth of damage. She wasn't too bright. Hopped up on drugs, speeding."

"How fast?"

"Oh, maybe eighty, or ninety. I was trying to turn left into the Y parking lot—she came around and tried to pass me as I turned. Creamed the front of the van."

"And you weren't hurt?"

"My shoulder aches sometimes, but I wasn't hurt. Neither was she apparently."

"Accidents are so awful."

"The thing about mine was that the woman was really attractive, really beautiful. Crude, but beautiful. Can you imagine it?"

"Yes."

"She's young of course—that's why she was speeding."

"You know who she is?"

"We exchanged I.D.s. We had to. The fire trucks and ambulances came."

"Was she hurt?"

"I said she wasn't"

"But there were ambulances."

"Right, and they took her away, but I think she was faking it-- trying to play down her own speeding and her recklessness."

"What?"

"She was pretending to be hurt so people wouldn't be thinking much that she actually caused the accident. Her crazy driving put everyone at risk. But another woman said she'd testify. She saw the whole thing and she knew the Camaro was out of control. And a kid came later on a bicycle and said the Camaro had passed him doing over a hundred. So there was no question which insurance would pay off," Owen said.

"She was driving like a demon. I wonder why."

"Probably bored. Or maybe her boyfriend was waiting. It was his car. Maybe he was going to beat her."

"No, I think she was afraid something would catch up with her," Owen's mother said, probing the end of the bed with her right hand to keep steady as she slowly flopped over into the covers.

"Yeah, maybe her boyfriend. He wasn't too pleased with the damage. Far worse than mine, I bet."

"Maybe she just wanted to get out of her current life. Maybe she couldn't imagine going on with it, whatever it was, and therefore took a severe risk. Drove like a demon, hoping she'd lose control. What's her boyfriend like?"

"Don't know. Never met him. Only talked once to his insurance agent."

"Do you like Barrett?"

"Yeah, sure. He seems a pretty nice guy."

"He's made a big difference during all this illness."

"I'm sure he has."

"He has. Well, goodnight, son. A don't worry too much over the girl's attractiveness. That fades you know."

"I guess for women it does." Owen said, and smiled.

"Very amusing," his mother answered. "I'm speaking the truth. It fades. Need for closeness doesn't fade though. You'll find somebody. But probably not somebody in a red Camaro. Goodnight."

In Anise's room Owen leafed through the Victoria's Secret catalogs, and imagined he could contrive some way to see Deirdre again, some less traumatic accidental collision. Maybe in the supermarket, although he could not imagine her shopping in such a place. More likely a disco or bar some night. More likely still, not at all. Maybe he'd just call again and be a bit more suave on the phone. But he knew she'd hardly give him the time for suavity. It would take a rash and willful, crunching accident to bring them together again. And he understood it was impossible for such a conjunction of forces to happen.

As he turned out the light he noticed a dull orange stain on back corner of the marble slab under his father's desk light. And in the dropping, absolute darkness he imagined and immediately dismissed, with aching longing, the enviable purposefulness of his mother and Barrett.

6

The Toughest Bar in Worcester

IN THE LAST, MOST profitable act of his Brahmin life Walter Jelliffe convinced his son, Waldo, to marry Suzan Corcoran, the slightly unhinged daughter of Worcester's richest family. That union brought Waldo the one enterprise he could fathom and embrace: publisher of Worcester's "alternative" weekly newspaper, *The New Worcester Spy*. Thus did Mayflower power fuse with the apparently limitless acquisitions flowing from Corcoran Abrasives. The linkage generated a certain amount of friction, and the titular Walter had been characteristically blunt with his son: "Anyone who marries for money earns every penny of it, but let's face it, there's *sweat-earnings* versus *suck-up earnings*. And from what I've seen of you, Waldo, the latter seems more natural, more in line with your tastes." There was a wondrous gentleness in the squeeze the old man applied to his son's shoulder and mind.

"I'll work at it, Daddy," Waldo replied. And he did. In the early years of the marriage Waldo spent hours on the fifth floor of Worcester Memorial Hospital's psych ward, listening to Suzan explain how she had made him rope sandals, and beaded leather wallets. He kept her on her lithium and constantly reassured her that given her situation she could have married almost anyone in Worcester–that he was in fact only the best of a long line of suitors. He worked hard to get her admitted to his luncheon club, The Worcester Club. It was largely through his efforts that women were eventually permitted even in the smoking rooms.

Waldo also worked hard at his publisher position–though he easily understood–as did all Jelliffes, that real work must be accomplished by others; his position and ownership was –and the phrase was his proudest editorial achievement–"residually iconic." He symbolized the sanctification of achievement by the "old line" in town. It was Walter Jelliffe himself who reiterated, after sufficient sherry, what he called John Keats' finest declaration: "A gentleman is one who is not wholly preoccupied with getting on." So Waldo, following Walter's lead, left actual actions, decisions, rewrites–in short, "getting-on" to others. He enjoyed being the final voice, never invoked, the absolute ruler whose only task was to meet the public and every now and then come up with a "brilliant feature proposal." The job left him gobs of time for slow luncheons at the club, side trips to Bermuda, early dinners with Suzan, month-long stays with her at various installations of sound mind and body. Waldo immensely enjoyed the latitude he had with *The Spy's* staff. He was at once the daffy uncle on the premises and the Zeus of certain death if you didn't play along . He was at *The Spy*, as in life itself, to be indulged. Indulgence came certainly with the Jelliffe name enforced with Corcoran monetary muscle.

Now in his fiftieth year Waldo Jelliffe had not given up the khakis of his swell collegiate life, nor the thin sweaters or cashmere blazers. He wore, as if in anticipation of his retirement years, and in recollection of his golden youth, New Balance running shoes or Timberland high tops in reverence for his New England roots even if, he noted at the club bar one night, the labor was not exactly Brahmin on Batam Island (where the shoes were made) perhaps a little swarthy even, and certainly dirt cheap. He was proud of his trip to Batam Island off the Malaysian coast, prouder still of his one single byline feature: "The Worcester/Batam Connection" in which he lovingly recorded the barracks lives of those exploited Southeast Asian laborers who sent everything they earned back home to China, India, the Philippines or wherever. Waldo had liked the spicy food and hammering Malaysian sun; he admired the way things ran so promptly and cleanly in Singapore. Worcester could learn a lot from ASEAN his one article maintained. And Kuala Lumpur was the one city on the planet he could emigrate to, he told the younger staffers and interns at *The Spy*, if circumstances should ever require him to leave Worcester. It interested him sometimes to wonder what those circumstances might be. Could he be a secret serial killer, filleting young women with one of Chef Tony's lifetime knives? He saw the knives advertised often enough on T.V., and once he had called the 800 number to inquire which of the knives would be best for gutting girls. "Be serious," the operator replied. "You want one set or two?"

Lately he spent more and more time with the younger staffers and interns since they only imperfectly understood his irrelevance. He was for them, the owner, the publisher, the ultimate authority, who merely husbanded his power by never displaying it. They did not understand what lineage could and could not do. And they responded enthusiastically to his rare proposals. And a few of them grasped that it was through Waldo that their own ideas could percolate in *The Spy's* system.

Thus it was not exactly clear who thought the feature up but Waldo certainly embraced the great pub crawl search for "The Toughest Bar in Worcester." And he began the deliberations with what he knew was the central point:

"Look, you have to have a standard, a comparison point on toughness. You've got to have a clear idea of what you mean by 'toughest.' What is the essence of 'toughness' and where do you find it? If you can point to one bar as 'tough,' then you can say X or Y exceeds that standard by such and such a factor and therefore it is not yet, 'The toughest Bar in Worcester.' And surprise of surprises, I can give us the standard: the old Valhalla Bar on Summer Street."

"It's gone–they built the new police station on the site," someone answered

"I know that, but its perishing makes it the perfect standard. No one can really say what it was on the scale of toughness. We can establish one ourselves. Besides, when I taught at the old jail, inmates told me it was the toughest bar in town. You could always be guaranteed a fight if you went in. That's toughness. Maybe we should put a time factor into the equation. Whadya think?"

"Art's Diner on West Boylston Street. The Huns hang out there."

"The Brass Helmut on Main Street-—Hispanic gangs."

"Any place on Green Street. Vietnamese gangs all over the place there."

Waldo objected, "We need more work on the standard. On criteria. Give me criteria. Something to sink our teeth into. Something the lunchpails will understand."

Waldo tended to regard those who worked for a living as "lunchpails," although the term disappointed and discouraged Walter Jelliffe.

"I still think we need a time constraint, "Waldo said. "You have to engage in actual fisticuffs within, say, nine minutes of entry. How does that sound?"

"You'll need a time keeper," Lewis Walling said, the most senior of the interns. There was a trace of whining sarcasm in his tone.

Waldo looked carefully at him, then finally said, "And a nifty stop watch, I suppose."

"And a hostility quotient," Walling continued, "maybe made up of equal parts rage, envy, insecurity, belief God is on your side."

"Lunchpail," Waldo answered.

"And we'd need bodyguards, people to do the actual fighting–either that or a year of combat training before we start the crawl."

Waldo and Suzan had no children, and Waldo had the habit of adopting one of the interns as the son he was convinced he didn't want. Lewis Walling was the latest in his adoptions–three previous ones had migrated to graduate school or Rhode Island papers. One became an editor in New Haven.

"Look, Walling, you like to throw log jams on the fire. I know that, but we can easily find a few thugs to back us up in testing the hostility. You probably know some yourself—football players or Rugby freaks."

"I do."

Part II: Mid-Stream

"Good, then let's not lock down over trivia. We need criteria-perfect criteria. A fight in nine minutes is a good start, but just a start."

"The first thirty seconds is crucial. True toughness signals itself right out of the gate. If you can't find a hostile phrase, look, gesture in 30 seconds, the place fails. We need a play book of gestures and phrases–that can be part of the article." Walling said, warming to the task.

"What about ethnicity?" Waldo asked.

"Meaning what?" Walling answered.

"Meaning should we stipulate a certain homogeneity as key to hostility. It's a Latino bar and we walk in and there's looks and so on. Does that qualify? Does the toughness have to go beyond resentment of outsiders? Isn't that natural and therefore discountable?"

"So it has to be a WASP bar?"

"Don't be stupid." Waldo said. "We're looking for an add-on factor—something that can begin in ethnic resentment but quickly boils over into generalized hatred, a pure viciousness aimed out of the soul of bile."

"The soul of bile," Walling repeated. "The soul of bile. Something that comes out of generations of repression? The end product of remembering that this town once was the center of New England, a palace of wire manufacturing –the barbed wire kingdom of the world and then, and then, the ugly descent as Swedes gave way to Italians and Irish and then to southeast Asians—wire to plastic, to gutted factories, abandoned mills, thence to boutiques and finally to plywood—so that everybody carries around a longing for some imagined time of prosperity. What begins as resentment for skin color ends as boiling rage and blame for loss of autonomy—all over some local IPA or Miller Lites? Is that it?"

"You catch on quick," Waldo laughed. "And always measured against the imagined slugfests at the old Valhalla."

"We seek the new Valhalla," Walling answered.

"Exactly!" Waldo said, "That's our title–'Seeking the new Valhalla.' Get us gladiators."

"I can get Singleton, Navy ROTC cadet commandant at Holy Cross–lots of rage just below the bellowing surface, and five or six Rugby players Singleton knows."

"Not five or six. One. One from the scrum. One large one from the scrum. Singleton plus one. Just adequate to get us out alive," Waldo smiled.

2.

The Spy's offices were on the sixth floor of a restored building on Front Street overlooking Worcester Commons. The freshly sand blasted facade of the building was directly across from the parched earth commons, grassless and flecked with grey scraps of winter snow. There was a large reflecting pool, utterly empty save for residue clumps of ice/snow and several half-crushed soda cans. Beyond the empty pool was a small graveyard with slightly twisted or turned headstones from the 18th century. And beyond the graveyard was a mammoth horse and soldier statue for the Spanish American war, prancing upward, kicking its hooves toward the plywooded and abandoned downtown aptly named Commons Fashion Outlet Mall.

When Walling and Singleton entered the Spy Building, along with Ralph (the one from the scrum) they all hurried past the little lobby area with its matching leather loveseats. Singleton had honed in on the marble sheathing over the three elevators beyond the lobby and seemed intent on reaching the seventh floor before anyone else. Walling admired Singleton's focus in this and all matters–no time to lose, no enemy too strong to be confronted, the perfect protector on any search for the toughest bar anywhere.

But Waldo from his leather loveseat headed Singleton and the rest off: "We're here ready for the charge, way ahead of you," he said, standing up and motioning to the woman still on the loveseat. "Suzan, meet our bodyguards."

Singleton, a gangly fellow probably 6 '2" or 6' 3," with a military brush cut and very thick black rimmed glasses was non-plused by Suzan's presence. How could you find boxing action with a woman in the entourage? The new Valhalla, a term Singleton cherished when Walling told it to him, might not have even a spot for visiting women. And on a mission women would only prove more vulnerable and difficult—didn't all his commanders acknowledge as much, although publicly they might speak quite contrarily about the admission of women into combat.

Suzan Jelliffe stood up, a delicately coiffured woman of 50, still quite thin with a longish face, too large a nose, and disturbingly vacant look to her face as if she were constantly imagining something beyond the apparent focus point of her eyes. A doorway perhaps through which would come something more interesting than things at hand? Waldo took her hand and said, "She's brought the camera."

"The camera?" Walling asked.

"Of course," Suzan said, suddenly and archly, "to record these events that alter and illuminate our time, together. Our little voyage into places where no one else has ever gone."

"The frolic spaces for the lunchpails," said Waldo, taking Suzan's hand.

"I thought we were hitting bars," Ralph the rugby player said.

"You'll do," Waldo said to him. "You'll do nicely. Solid, and can take a punch. He can take a punch. See Suzy, he can take a punch." And Waldo slapped him on the arm.

Walling said, "So we don't have to go upstairs?"

"Nope," Waldo said, "She's got the camera right here." He pointed to Suzan's fabric bag. "I had a hole cut for the lens–takes digital pictures–we'll get everything and nobody will notice."

Singleton said, "I hope it's not too valuable."

"The publisher will pay." Waldo answered. "Now let's head over to The Brass Helmut and see if we can stir something up."

"This will be exciting," Suzan said, and she took Walling's arm.

But the Brass Helmut was not exciting. It was nearly vacant—a smallish brown rectangle with a bar along the outside edge and only two very elderly fellows on stools near the door. The bartender was a young Latino woman who seemed to recognize Ralph.

"This place smells terrible," Suzan said, loud enough.

The Toughest Bar in Worcester

"Maybe we're too early," Walling said.

"Look, I can get something going, "Singleton said. "I know I can. If that's what you want."

Waldo answered: "It's not what we want –it's what the venue offers. Don't you get it? We're here just to evaluate what the ambience is."

"Ambience?" Ralph said.

"How fast we get into combat," Walling said.

"The smell is just awful," Suzan said. "Has someone thrown up? I don't think we should stay here."

"We've got to wait the nine minutes," Singleton said, "to make the experiment valid."

"Fuck validity," Waldo shouted. "We're outta here!"

They went out back onto Main Street, past the Beacon pharmacy and on toward some Irish bars further south.

"I really couldn't drink in there. I really couldn't" Suzan said. "I know the experiment won't be valid, and I'm sorry, really sorry about that, but I just couldn't stay there a minute longer. The smell was ghastly, just ghastly."

"No worries, pet, "Waldo answered." The place didn't measure up. That was clear from the minute we entered."

"We didn't give it enough time, "Singleton said. "We need to stick to the plan."

"Shut up," Waldo said. "I'm running this operation."

"And I can't really do much walking. It's too cold. I should have brought a heavier coat," Suzan said. "I'm sorry but I can't really walk much more."

"No worries, pet." Waldo said. "We'll go back to the garage and get the van. I've got the best place in mind."

"It's got to have people in it. We're too early, "Walling said.

"Maybe," Waldo conceded, "but that can't be helped now. We're launched. Let's get the van."

"We're not thinking clearly," Singleton said. "If we need the van we're going beyond the periphery of our experiment. You can't drive to the toughest bar–that means it could be anyplace. We're trying to establish the toughest bar in Worcester, a specific place."

"Yes," Suzan said slowly, " a very specific place. With boundaries of possibility."

"Nonsense," Waldo said. "Within the city limits, just too damn far to walk. The van will be okay."

"I don't think so," Singleton insisted.

"You're not being paid to think."

"Are we being paid?" Ralph said.

"One way or another, "Waldo said, "now tell him to shut up." Waldo pointed to Singleton, who had taken off his heavy glasses and was rubbing the sides of his nose.

Waldo drove them in the van up Belmont Street to the very edge of Worcester's limits. Then he turned left, went up another hill and parked behind a large house, the first floor of which was labeled, *Bronzino's Bar*.

"I've heard of this place," Walling said.

"It's too close to the outskirts," Singleton said.

"Ralph, tell him to shut up." Waldo said.

Suzan said, "I feel nauseous. Let's stay outside a while, in the cold. That helps. "

"Maybe we should have walked here," Singleton said.

"Walling, where did you find this clown?" Waldo asked.

"How can we measure hostility out there,"Walling pointed to *Bronzino's*, "If we're coming at each other here?"

"We don't need internal antagonism," Suzan said. "We certainly don't need that."

"We need a goddamn challenge, so let's go get one," Waldo said, pushing ahead of the group.

3.

Inside *Bronzino's* dirty green wall-to-wall carpet gave way to grey linoleum in the expanse of space that must have been living room, dining, room kitchen shot-gunned together. There were five round, heavily varnished, walnut tables with thick heavily varnished chairs in the space. Three of the tables were filled with patrons—overweight women and men, pitchers of beer, smudged glasses, peanut bowls half empty, shells littering the table tops.

"This could be a Knights of Columbus Bingo party," Waldo said quietly, disappointed.

"I'll get us a pitcher of beer," Singleton said, as if in expiation. "Sit here." He pulled out a hefty dark chair for Suzan.

"This seems like a family bar," Waldo said, sitting down and apparently irritated that Singleton had taken charge of the next minutes.

"I wonder if there's such a thing as a family bar?" Walling said.

"In London, at the better pubs, you can sit with your family," Suzan said. "Sometimes it's so nice to sit with your children in the back garden area of the pub or in a side room away from the noise."

"You have children?" Ralph asked.

"No," Waldo answered. "Only staffers."

"I went with my father to pubs in Highgate and Hampstead. They were lovely." Suzan continued.

"I'm looking at these people and I can't see hostility at all. In fact I'm wondering why I was given the name of this place. It's like a low class, lunchpail bridge convention or something. Strictly lunchpail. And now we have to wait through a pitcher of beer. Probably crappy beer too."

Singleton came back with the beer and five small glasses. He poured a round and said, "Here's to the memory of the Valhalla. Maybe Worcester no longer has a toughest bar."

Waldo countered: "In KL –that's Kuala Lumpur–" He paused looking at Ralph, then added. "That's Malaysia, Kuala Lumpur Malaysia. The capital city. You can't get any bacon. It's a Muslim country. You can't get pork. Course, you can, but only in the Chinese sections of KL. But on the breakfast menus you'll find a reference to 'bacon substitute.' You know what that is?"

Ralph said immediately, "No."

"Well, it's thin strips of veal, strips fried up like bacon. And delicious, but more expensive than bacon."

"Not many things more expensive than bacon lately," Suzan said.

"Right you are, pet. Right you are. This place shows me nothing. Who recommended this place?"

"We've got to finish our beer and wait our nine minutes," Singleton said.

"The hell we do," Waldo said.

"Well, we ought to," Singleton continued. "The experiment has to be fully done and completely replicable."

"I like that word, replicable," Suzan said, savoring the syllables. "Rep lick ah bull."

"In the barracks on Batam Island the workers sleep in hammocks, sometimes four tiers high," Waldo said.

"Tiers?" Ralph asked.

"Tears indeed," Suzan answered. "You should hear him and see his tears over the exploited workers of Batam Island."

"Okay," Waldo said, getting up. "We're outta here."

"I paid for the beer," Singleton said.

"Tell me at the end of the evening," Waldo said.

"Tell you what?"

"How much you shelled out to keep this crew fat and happy."

"We're not so happy," Walling said.

"We're outta here," Waldo said again.

"Maybe we should try some place with Huns around," Singleton suggested.

"Maybe you should wait for your orders, "Waldo said.

"Yes!" added Ralph, draining the beer pitcher.

In the van Waldo said, "I've got one more place recommended. On Park Avenue. Maybe a kind of immediate 'post-college' place. Called the Foo Bar."

"I know it," Singleton shouted.

"Oh, he knows it," Waldo echoed. "But I'm worried we're losing our focus. We're not just going to bars. We're trying to find the toughest bar in Worcester. Isn't that what we're trying to do?"

"Who cares?" said Suzan.

"Our readers, pet. The ones who keep us in Bermuda when we need it most."

"Like now," said Walling.

"Oh, not like now," Suzan continued, "certainly not now, when we're collecting all this important data about tough bars in Worcester."

"Yes," said Ralph.

"I like you," Suzan said. "You're affirming."

"One from the scrum is always affirming." Walling said.

The Foo Bar had a dark red glow. The bar stools were filled, but the occupants seemed too well dressed for toughness, and too preoccupied with the Red Sox game on the two large television screens bracketing the bar. The noise level, however, was promising. Shouting filled the low-ceilinged room and the red lamps with their translucent red shades supplied the proper motivation for fisticuffs.

"We can get something going here," Singleton said, drawing extra chairs to the tiny round table beyond the left end of the bar.

"You've got it backwards and I'm getting tired of pointing that out," Waldo said.

Suzan said, relaxing back into the chair Singleton pushed further under her, "Tell us about Batam Island. You know, about the sleeping arrangements."

"Don't get cute," Waldo said. "It's not you."

"Oh, but it's you," Suzan sing-songed back to Waldo.

Walling brought over gin and tonics. "Imagine it's summer," he said.

"Beer and gin doesn't work," Singleton said.

"Let's see," Suzan said. She took a long drink. "Yes, it can work."

Ralph finished his drink in one long swig, and went to the bar to get another.

"Let's go back over the criteria," Waldo said, slumping a bit in his chair, scuffing a bit his Timberlands along the chocolate, stained and worn carpet.

When he got back and before he sat down, Ralph said a bit too loudly, "I hate the Red Sox."

Singleton smiled and nodded at Waldo.

"You've got to remember the criteria." Waldo said.

"If it's not around, you've got to make it happen," Singleton answered.

"The Red Sox suck," Ralph said, again too loudly. A few bar stools spun slowly at the sentiment, turning away from the spring-training, pre-season game.

4.

A distant segment of the bar lifted up and a burly fellow in a grey sweatshirt slowly walked through the opening.

"Here it comes," Singleton said, joyous at the prospect.

He came to within a foot of their table. "You nice people see *Roadhouse* with Patrick Swayze?" the burly fellow asked, taking off his baseball hat and holding it politely with both hands in front of his waist.

"Yes," Walling answered.

"Then you remember Patrick's little suggestion to his bouncers– 'be —nice.' So I'm in my Patrick Swayze 'be-nice' phase, just asking you to tone it down. Keep it down, since there happen to be a lot of Red Sox fans here, as you might expect, wouldn't you? Anybody might expect that."

"Yeah, there' are dicks everywhere," Ralph said, smiling.

"I'm going to be 'be-nice' and overlook that disappointing observation."

"Up yours," Ralph said.

"I can tell you want me to leave my 'be-nice' persona and become mother-fucking Steven Seagal, is that it?"

"Sure," Ralph answered.

"In *Out for Justice* mother-fucking Seagal puts a cue ball in a handkerchief and slugs teeth all over the pool table. And I like that a lot. All the time he's shouting 'This is your trophy,' holding up his badge. I like that mother-fucking Seagal."

"Hey," Ralph suddenly shouted, "Why don't you curb your foul mouth. Don't you know there's classy cunt here?" He looked at Suzan.

The bar, the game on the television, the announcers in their booths suddenly fell silent at Ralph's proclamation. Red glow grew a notch. Singleton eased up from his chair. The baseball hat fell quietly to the floor. For a very long time, it seemed, no one could think of anything to say, and later Waldo would note the presence of what he called "the very ambivalent pause," the stop-time sequence in which violence or retreat could weigh the balance and flop one way or the other. "That has to be factored in somehow—that moment, the propensity of that moment one way or the other. That's the damn criterion we've been looking for. Some settings, some ambiances stir things one way or another. We've got to break that down, itemize its factors and provide some quantitative measure. That's what we mean by the toughest bar in town."

Ever the deflectionist Walling interceded with an offer, "Here let me pick up your hat." He eased out of his chair, dropped to his haunches and reached for the hat just covering the bouncer's left shoe.

"That's a nice gesture." The fellow said, slowly. "It puts me in the mind of tolerating this asshole," he gestured toward Ralph, who in rising up tossed the table directly at the knees of the bouncer and over Walling's ducking head. The edge of the table cracked directly into the bouncer's kneecaps sounding as if a truck had run over chicken bones. The large center leg of the table drove into Walling's backbone with such force that Walling threw up on the shoes of the bouncer. Not content with this mayhem, Ralph grabbed the bouncers short hair and slammed his head into the top of the tilted table, not once, not twice, but four machine-gunned times. Teeth spilled out, blood flowed down the table top and into the vomit on the floor. The sound of teeth skittering and Walling gagging , coughing and retching filled the room.

Waldo shouted with delight, "One from the scrum delivers. And how! "

Suzan began taking digital pictures of the cascaded table.

"Jesus!" Singleton said, "someone call an ambulance. For God's sake call an ambulance."

The young woman behind the bar screamed, "They've killed Eric."

"Not yet," said Ralph. "Not yet, but soon!" He kicked the table over so that it came to rest atop the bouncer's unconscious body, two feet beyond Walling, still kneeling and retching.

"Wait a minute," Waldo shouted. "We're done. It's over. We're done. No more. Nothing more!"

The bar stools emptied as patrons ran for the front door.

"You've killed Eric." The woman insisted again, to the vacant room.

Singleton dragged the table off. "No he's breathing fine, just bloodied. He'll be fine. But, Mr. Jelliffe, I'm not sure how we'll put all this back together."

"Yes, how will we assemble it," Suzan said cheerily. "How does it go back to the way it was?"

"Walling, you okay?" Waldo asked.

"It will take a lot of lawyers to make everything right again," Suzan said, taking more pictures.

"Pet, put away the digital. We need to address the problems at hand," Waldo said evenly.

"Walling, can you speak?"

"Yes, but no wind, no breath."

"Take it easy," Singleton said. "You'll get your breath back. Can you move your arms?"

Walling lifted his arms.

"You'll be fine," Singleton said.

"A whole floor of lawyers," Suzan said. "Maybe more. But maybe we can sue. . . ."

"Now you're thinking, Pet. Of course we can sue. How damn aggressive can a bouncer get, coming directly at us? Shouting obscenities. Challenging us. Over some stupid game. Calling us out over some innocent, completely innocent observation aimed at no one. No one at all."

"It smells bad in here, "Suzan said.

Waldo said, "Ralph, take Mrs. Jelliffe back to the office and wait there for us. We'll manage everything here, Pet. Don't worry. It'll make a helluva feature."

5.

That night Waldo dreamed of Batam Island. In khaki shorts and mint Teva sandals he walked among the sleeping hammocks of barracks 21–7 and counted for his own collection of possible feature material the rather low number of mosquito nettings surrounding some of the hammocks. The air was dense, mucid, sweat-inducing, so that the polyester of his quayabera shirt (in French blue) clung to his back. Waldo thought, "These are my people–young brown, breathing easily in the hot night." Arms were flung out to him; he had to swivel by several just to reach the far end of the barracks. In the morning they'd each eat a bowl of rice topped by a raw egg. They didn't give a damn about *The Spy*, had no longings for any part of the Worcester Club, envied him nothing of Suzan's largess. Instead, *The Spy* had given him a translator, a wiry forty-year-old with thick black hair somehow knotted in back. In baggy canvas pants and with a lemon colored T shirt the fellow was, Waldo convinced himself, the very personification of Lunch Pail. He promptly dubbed him that and was doubly pleased that the fellow took no insult from the nickname–apparently assumed it was an American term of endearment.

Waldo heard the fellow say from a corner of the barracks, "Captain, what are you doing here?"

"Checking on the troops, LP. Just checking." Waldo answered.

"Checking for what?"

"For conviction, LP. For conviction. I can measure who will get out, who will blossom."

"Blossom?"

"Grow, LP, grow. Enlarge, marry well, acquire, maybe, maybe only acquire."

"Acquire?"

"Buy stuff. . .own stuff. Not flip-flops, LP, but real sandals. Real leather, or maybe real velcro."

"I know velcro."

"I'm sure you do, LP. I'm sure you do. It's what keeps us attached, isn't it?"

"Attached?"

"It was a joke, Lunch Pail, just a joke. "

"You're always joking, and I don't like joking. I don't like it. I don't understand it."

"LP, if you can't laugh, you can't live."

"I don't like joking."

"Get over it, Lunch Pail. It makes the world go round."

But LP, drawing closer, had brought up a small mallet from behind him. He tapped it on his palm. Then inverted it so that he held the rubber end, the handle extending toward Waldo. He jabbed it into Waldo's chest.

"Hey what are you doing?"

"I don't like joking."

"Good, LP. I understand that."

"I don't like it." He jabbed the handle harder into Waldo, shifted downwards toward his sternum. Then in a savage strike drew back and rammed the end into Waldo's stomach. Waldo doubled over, heard something snap in his lungs, saw a flash camera go off, heard Suzan say, "Oh my! That's not good. That's bad," felt his knees buckle, was aware that the wide boards of the barracks floor had risen strangely to embrace him. LP neatly flipped the handle in his hand so that the mallet end was now in striking position. Waldo cocked his head and presented his left temple for the fatal blow, but woke up before Lunch Pail could bludgeon him. Waldo thought, "God! I love ASEAN."

7

We Say 4 Is Bigger than, Larger than, More than 3

Dr. Arnold Pearson was a near legendary sports orthopedic surgeon on the west coast of Florida. He purchased 600 feet of Gulf frontage on Gordon Key and built a house on stilts 120 feet beyond the highest tide mark on his beach. He had two children and wife who had her own dental practice. He had three cars, all parked under his stilt house. Once each week in the late afternoon he played at least one hard set of tennis at the Hane Country Club, and on Saturday mornings he ran a tennis clinic at the Hane Public Courts behind Hane High School.

It was there he met Kevin Small who would destroy the doctor's admirable life. Small was the court's caretaker and lived in a yellow trailer a stone's throw from the High School. He had arthritis, with strange knobs growing out of his thin elbows, and weirdly bunched fingers that made dragging the giant broom with which he daily swept the clay courts very difficult and tiring. Sometimes Small's son, a severely retarded boy of 14, stunted and with a hunchback, helped him by walking behind the broom and picking up the gum wrappers that had evaded the bristles. More often, however, the boy simply rocked back and forth standing by the lone, cracked and rusted, vinyl-topped white table at courtside. The boy found the motion evidently soothing and Dr. Pearson sometimes admired the child's ability to detach entirely from the brooming, the noisy competition of the tennis team, and Pearson's own sweaty breathing to keep up with the tennis players he advised. The boy and the surgeon sometimes stood side by side as Pearson shouted instructions out onto the courts. Dr. Pearson felt a kinship with the boy, Bobby Small, and that became evident to Kevin Small.

For that very reason one particular chilly Saturday morning Small poured out his fears to Dr. Pearson.

"Would you, could you help me with Bobby? I've tried any number of tutors, but they all gave up. I need someone to teach him basic math, basic reading, basic anything so he can find some kind of work and be self-supporting. Otherwise I don't know how he'll live after we're gone. He can't tell time yet. He needs to be able to tell time. He needs basic math skills. Do you think you could spend time with him–any amount. He needs a different voice explaining things to him. The tutors tried but they all gave up."

"It's not really my field," Dr. Pearson said rather slowly, thinking about it. "I have no experience teaching. None whatsoever."

"But the others all had the experience, the training, everything, but they failed. So expertise doesn't count for my Bobby. I don't know what counts, so I'm willing to try anything."

"Let me think about it, maybe consult someone about it," Dr. Pearson said, feeling strangely that somehow a steel plate had slipped its way into his side, between his fifth and sixth rib.

Was it a crick in his back muscles, or in fact had something knifed its way in? He felt along the right side of his rib cage, but there was no porcelain handle, no three riveted steel blade pushing into his lung.

That night Dr. Pearson mentioned Bobby to his wife.

"You ought to help the boy. Besides, teaching him might cut the stress of your regular work. It's pretty different from laparoscopic surgery, isn't it?" she said, smiling at him with brilliantly white teeth.

"I wonder if you really have my best interests at heart?" Dr. Pearson said.

"I always, always, do."

"Of course you do."

2.

The next Saturday afternoon, Dr. Pearson met Kevin Small's wife, Ann, a very short woman with one damaged eye and chin line that signaled some congenital deformity. She spoke with a phlegmy rasp that Pearson found hard to follow. But evidently she was thanking him for agreeing to teach Bobby. But he hadn't agreed. She pointed to a grey metal folding chair beside a blue card table set up in the trailer's center. Bobby sat in another chair next to the one she indicated the doctor should take. He sighed and sat down. Kevin and Ann left the trailer with anticipatory smiles that irritated the doctor.

"Well, Bobby, I guess we should get acquainted."

"Get acquainted," Bobby said immediately and in the tones Pearson had used. There was a certain tiredness in his voice.

"How old are you?"

"How old are you," Bobby repeated, "I am fourteen years old." He paused then said, a bit louder, "I am fourteen years old." He began rocking his head and watching carefully to see what Dr. Pearson's facial expression indicated.

But Pearson was staring deeply into Bobby's rather shifty eyes and thinking, there's a person inside this child. It was as if the doctor had just torn open a shoulder and begun to probe for the strained or severed ligaments surrounding a broken rotator cuff. There is a person inside this rocking child, the doctor heard himself saying in some very quiet segment of his own body, a child pumping along involuntarily like his own heart. I'd like to engage that child; I'd like to get to know that child. I need only clamp aside some interfering muscles, sift through faulty ligaments and sow things back together.

"I am a surgeon," Pearson said.

"Surgeon," Bobby echoed.

"Yes, so, so. . . ." Pearson lost his train of thought. The child he imagined he could engage had fled, or at least what evidence of him came unglued from the boy's face, that seemed adrift, suddenly a mask awaiting outside painting to restore expression.

"So, your father has asked me to teach you about basic math."

"Basic math," Bobby repeated, apparently delighted once again to say the phrase.

"Yes, basic math," Pearson echoed. "Basic math, and maybe basic time-telling." And he thought, that was a stupid mistake: introducing a second task, second intellectual challenge. "Well maybe not basic time-telling."

"Not telling time today," Bobby said, slowly.

So he could sort through dual concepts, dual propositions, Pearson thought, perked up by that recognition, heartened by it.

3.

"It was a breakthrough of cognition, and that gave me unimaginable hope," Dr. Pearson said to his wife later that night. "It was like I drank slow-acting poison because I really believed, actually, really believed that I could communicate and change his abilities. I could implant little seeds of competence that would speed him along to self-sufficiency. Now I realize how foolish I was, how stupidly ambitious."

"All that after one visit?"

"You think I've piled up too much?"

"You've said it. Besides, stupid ambition has been your sentinel all along."

"Just as you've been the sensible lodestar yanking us both back into mediocrity."

"You love summarizing without me. Why don't you put some of that energy into helping Bobby, and easing Kevin's pain."

"So I should continue the meetings?"

"You dream of planting seeds, so proceed," she said with a nod and then an afterthought: "Just leave me out of it."

"How can I leave you out of it, when you so marvelously weave me back into it?"

"You'll find a way."

We Say 4 Is Bigger than, Larger than, More than 3

"You have to admit it's a fascinating problem—like turning a sow's ear into a silken purse."

His wife smiled and said, "Judgmental is always riding for a fall."

But there was no fall in his next meeting with Bobby. It seems almost too easily that the boy could distinguish the larger tower of stacked pennies from the shorter tower.

"So we say the tower here," Dr. Pearson pointed to the stack of 15 pennies, "is larger than, or taller than, or bigger than or more than the stack here," he pointed to the shorter stack of 4 pennies.

"Bigger than," Bobby repeated smiling, almost laughing.

"Yes, yes! Which is the larger stack of pennies?"

"Stack of pennies."

"Yes. Stack of pennies, which one is the larger, or bigger stack?"

"The bigger or larger."

"Please point to the larger, or bigger, or taller stack."

Bobby pointed to the taller stack.

"Yes, yes, that's so great. So you've learned something. You now know when something is more than something similar."

"Something similar." Bobby repeated laughing. He started rocking in his narrow metal chair.

Pearson clamped down hard on the boy's left shoulder. "No need to rock now. You're just getting it. No rocking, please. No rocking." Pearson was surprised by the intensity of his voice.

"That hurts," Bobby said, looking away from Dr. Pearson.

"I'm sorry," Pearson said, quickly releasing his grip. "Sometimes I get carried away. When you're doing so well I get confused that you begin to rock as if you weren't doing well."

"You weren't doing well," Bobby echoed.

"But you are, and you were."

"Doing well."

"Okay, I think we can graduate to quarters. I'm going to put down a line of quarters and you can count each one as I put it down on the table. Can you do that?" Pearson put one quarter slowly on the blue vinyl.

Bobby said, "One."

"Good, great. And now the next one."

"One," said Bobby.

"Not exactly. That is number one there, this is the next quarter and we say it's number___"

"Not exactly," Bobby echoed.

"That number one and so this next is number _____"

Bobby, watching him carefully finally said, "Number two."

"Great! And this next one is number what?"

Bobby went back to rocking.

"Here's number one, here's number two, and here's number . . .. what?"

Still rocking Bobby began lolling his head around.

Pearson grabbed the boy's hand, extending the fingers. "Here's number one, here's two," he said pulling on each finger, "and therefore here's number ____"

"Three," Bobby said.

"Yes! Exactly! Three fingers and three quarters. Now I put down another line of quarters right underneath the line of three. Here's the first of the new line, or as we say, 'Number ___'"

"New Line," Bobby said enthusiastically.

"We say, 'Number One,'" Pearson said sternly correcting him.

"Number One," Bobby echoed.

"Which line is longer?" the doctor asked, discouragement suddenly flooding into him.

Bobby rocked more sharply.

"I've put a line of four quarters and underneath it I've put a line of ten quarters. A line of ten. Can you tell me which line is longer?"

"Which line is longer," Bobby smiled, rocking again.

"Yes, which is the longer line? The one here?" he pointed to the top line of three quarters on the blue vinyl, "Or here?" He pointed to the bottom line.

Bobby turned and stared a long time directly into Dr. Pearson's eyes. The look at once vacant and searching disturbed Pearson and he finally said. "It's okay, Bobby. It's more my fault than yours."

"More mine than yours." Bobby echoed, then he got up from his chair and quickly went outside where his parents we seated on Adirondeck chairs in the sunlight, and said "It's more my fault than yours. It's more my fault than yours."

4.

"You tried to move him along far too fast," his wife said a few nights later. "You always push things too fast.

"It would be nice to think so."

"Ah, your standard *weltschmertz,* your first love. Just don't let it affect your work."

"My work? Surgery or basic math?"

"Maybe that's the problem, a certain confusion."

Pearson thought about such a confusion. "Maybe you're right," he said. "It's sort of like an attenuated tendon, paper thin so that you think you could perhaps stretch it a bit more and re-attach it in some way that would preserve its working, but you're not sure you can grip it sufficiently to pull it into position without losing it entirely. I can imagine myself with just the slightest hold on some brain tissue trying to haul it into comprehension, but no, it's sliding away slipping deeper into some area I can't see. It's then I understand Kevin's desperation and his wife's funny smiling and mucusy mumbling, as if we're all three looking at the future and knowing it won't work, as if the boy is on the table and his brain spilling out onto the beige rubber gurney and we're there with spatulas and putty knives and working so hard to push stuff back into place. And then he sits up suddenly and starts throwing brain mater around the room, off the chrome mirrors and into the off-white walls."

"You seem to like your desperation of thinking about it. Could that be the problem.? You like the feeling you're failing and nothing can be done about that. The boy is showing you something you'd like to master, but you know you can't, and that's very liberating. You can only be your lousy, witless, self, out of any control."

"Yes. Yes, it's a helluva feeling. And I can truthfully tell him 'it's more my fault than his.' Because I simply don't know how to say easily and clearly, something is 'more than' something else. Maybe nothing is *more than* something else. Including 'fault.'" Pearson said slowly. "Including fault. Getting at that boy inside, like hunting around for a snapped tendon laparscopically, probing around and around hoping to find a white strand in the darkness and hook it so you could pull it back and find a way to reattach it. It was like that exactly. Exactly. But I couldn't fish it out, pull it off reattach it, it was so lost. There he was as inert as a flaccid muscle mass, yet with beguiling sensitivity to what he imagined I wanted him to say, to be in fact. But what did I want? He wasn't interested in grasping numbers; he wanted only to see in my reaction some approval for what he did or did not say. Words were only prompts for his evaluation of my reaction. Somewhere in that shoulder was a soul fast asleep and I couldn't wake it up, or maybe a brain waiting for a connector someplace."

"I wouldn't savor your failure too much, if I were you."

"If you were only me," Pearson answered softly. "If you were me, he'd assume your love, your constant approval, and quickly want to move toward something on his own. I really believe that, but he knows you're not me, and so he's stuck at getting my approval. I've got to find a way to love him apart from his grasp of numbers. Something *more than* I'm presently giving him. That's got to be my focus."

"Well, at least that's a new focus and we can remember our lives for a while again."

But Pearson did not hear bitterness in her whisper to him. He listened only to his sudden commitment to be more loving, more affirming to Bobby—elements he attempted in the next two sessions quite apart from the laborious business of comparing size or length or stacked heights to hammer home the concept of numbers.

He praised and patted the boy on his neck and shoulders for the slightest apparent attention given to the lesson. He reiterated how much he liked being in Bobby's company, how he found joy and real pleasure in Bobby's rocking presence.

We Say 4 Is Bigger Than, Larger Than, More Than 3

Still, at the end of each session Pearson left the yellow trailer blinking at the spectacular scarlets of the sunsets as if his blood had combined to generate the painted and swirling sky.

The boy's receptivity was impenetrable, perfectly transparent in its opaqueness. Gradually as Pearson drove back on the filled-in roadway past the artificially created keys, with their rows of immense Ocala block houses past the enormous public beach adjacent to Gordon Key he drifted into different imagined conversations with Bobby so that words floated between them as real thoughts, not markers of his own expression of approval and satisfaction. He imagined they talked about something other than numbers, something beyond bigger or larger or more than, so that Bobby could actually listen as Pearson told him about the niftiness of sunsets and the absurdity of appreciating that ending daily spectacle. In the hum of the near silent car engine it was as if they were encapsulated like the pelicans skimming the surface, complete and enshrined in the lilting flapless, smooth glide above the shimmering waters. But Pearson recognized he'd never get there, and that was too alluring a failure as his wife had simply said.

Two weeks later in the center of a moonless Wednesday night, at 2:45 a.m. he slipped out of bed mumbling something like "only taking a leak," and then sat in his Chrysler convertible beside the stilts imagining how easy it would be to drive at the lowest tide out to the sandbar a thousand feet from shore and wait there for the tide to come in. If he had bound his feet to the brake pedal using plastic handcuffs so easily available, and if then he had bound his wrists to the steering wheel, he'd be immobilized at the tide came in and gradually filled the vehicle. He imagined the gentle sea swelling through the floor boards and mats, easing over his feet and finally shorting out the radio playing the lovely trio music he imagined death generated. Water over his lap as he frantically sought some way to sever the plastic grip and knowing perfectly that he'd thought of everything, even the toenail clipper he kept in the unreachable glove compartment, till the relentless tide of Gordon Key came fully over the 120 feet he'd so carefully calculated for his dream home.

In the morning when he recounted his imagined exit from this life, his wife listened carefully, nodding between sips of coffee, and finally said, "You always told me you could recognize a surgeon by the way he tied his knots, but plastic cuffs don't use a knot, just an escalating wedge notch as you pull them tight. That's not very distinctive, nothing like a signature."

Part III

At the Falls

8

The Point Of The Hook

WHEN JOHN SPRADLIN RETIRED he understood all possessions were ashes, all attachments snapable, all memories dissolving. He liked the notion that his life like a vase was falling toward marble steps seventy-five floors below. He hoped before shattering to misunderstand what he'd read somewhere that consciousness was just a flicker between two voids—eternal emptiness before and eternal emptiness after. He heard his children's voices and attended to their needs, but increasingly death's tinnitus overcackled care. He kept sorting through memories trying to find the first moment of his recognition of the downward swoosh of comic despair.

And he fixed on the ten weeks of his 26th year when he met and fell under the suasion of Chief Easter and Bosunmate Moulton. Those weeks at the Sandy Hook's Coast Guard Lifeboat Station, a spit of land New Jersey sent out daringly into the Atlantic Ocean became, he now believed, the wrenching point. By then he had perceived his life as a diminishing set of doorways to bliss, each one requiring he believed, a leader to help him across the slippery tiles and beyond the water-scored lintels. By then he had come to understand that the U.S. government owned all of the choice beachfront land, whether in Florida, or Virginia, or New Jersey, Texas, California or Washington state. And in his late twenties he thought that entirely appropriate— he had succumbed to the easy thought that land in common was fairer than land in private hands. The earth was the Lord's and the fullness thereof and they that dwell there-in. There-in. There-in.

"There-in is a key phrase in our conception of where the Coast Guard should be going, where, in fact, it will go if we can find enough new recruits to the cause," Chief Easter said quickly to him a voice a notch or two above whisper, the white purity of his smoothly glistening cheek barely seven inches from Spradlin's nose, the scent of Old Spice aftershave swimming in the thick, salted afternoon air.

"I don't follow how 'there-in' explains anything about the new Guard."

"It's a kind of pun that you have to live into to fully grasp," Chief Easter said quietly. He was standing on the porch of Spradlin's barracks, and there were rounded pyramids of sand beyond his shoulders and beyond those an immense glistening blue/black sea. The brilliantly creased dress whites of Easter seemed a perfect contrast/complement to those distant waters. For a moment Spradlin imagined the Chief had walked in on top of that sea. Easter's voice had a crisp whisper-care to it that seemed, suddenly to Spradlin, to require genuflection. It seemed then, and now, that a voice deep inside Spradlin was quietly musing: "This man might be *the* leader." In any event, pay attention to him, for he seemed on a wavelength or a frequency unobtainable. How receptive I was then, Spradlin thought.

"A pun?"

"You know—there-in equals *they're in*, which they all will be after Chief Easter inspires them." Bosunmate Moulton said, putting his heavy arm around Spradlin's shoulders and involuntarily bending him forward. "You would do well, to listen to Chief Easter."

Moulton seemed fond of somewhat archaic expressions like "You'd do well to. . . . . ." or at a lower frequency, "speaking of intercoursing Petty Officers. . . . ." Spradlin knew Moulton was basically a thug, muscle to enforce whatever dictate Chief Easter might proclaim, but always in an arch way, never with scrappy hostility. Was that Easter's influence? Did Easter train thugs to sound like artificial gentlemen, Spradlin wondered.

Spradlin was familiar enough with barracks hierarchies. The boss needed a thug enforcer, an intimidator lap dog, always on the prowl to bite off resistance. Moulton seemed small for that task and Spradlin imagined there was someone else to handle a real challenge.

But Chief Easter seemed beyond challenge and that interested Spradlin. Whence came the authority, the command, the acquiescence, the charisma? Could it be the setting: thick white painted boards of the barracks, and classrooms, glossy orange/maroon linoleum floors full of the bulbous swirling strokes of endless floor buffers? And always a salty sea breeze. Sometimes Spradlin could imagine from the evening chill that he was on a mountain top, a flat peak with improbable sand pilings. And in the distance the soft sound of the roiling sea spreading its blue-black, tufted white panoply over the horizon. There was a delicious monasticism to the place. Rutted, sandy, single-lane passages separated the myriad buildings, lanes studded with sea grass and scrub bushes. And for the first two weeks it never rained. Instead, sun hammering turned the scene shimmering in Spradlin's watering eyes.

Moulton interrupted that reverie: "We reversed the booking. It's gone away. But there were things you never mentioned, and that disappointed us."

"What things?"

"Like you're throwing the hamburger away and storming off, even after the Ensign said you could finish before exiting. He showed you some kindness and you took offense."

"I didn't know it was an Officer's Country canteen."

"We understood that. We've overcome that violation. We interceded for you. The booking won't happen, but you weren't fully honest with us. In the New Guard honesty, full honesty, is foundational. We were very disappointed."

Sifting through it now, Spradlin imagined the precision of their language was part of their suasion. *Foundational* was a term to be savored in Spradlin's memory. It was a favorite of Chief Easter's. The heart must alter at a foundational level—changing the heart's architecture was a key to survival and beyond survival, to flourishing.

Didn't Chief Easter accentuate such thoughts, or were they in fact the sentiments—automatic and without any conviction—issued by a resident cardiologist looking after Spradlin's surprising infarction in his 62nd year?

"We defend our own, and aggressively. And I suspect the Ensign, hapless enforcer, had decided, when we asked him, not to cause trouble with us. We watch out for our own and that's known, accepted, respected here." Chief Easter said in his soft voice. "We're about laying the foundation for a new Guard and that's also respected here. We've earned that respect. You haven't—except through our intervention. But effective intervention requires absolute and full honesty. The new Guard defends its own but only if the whole situation is clear, totally clear. We've stopped your booking. Remember that, and use that memory to cleanse all of your future actions. We will protect you, just as we have in this case. But you must be honest with us. Nothing held back."

"No mental reservation," Spradlin had said, and that angered Moulton, who speared his fist and third knuckles deep into Spradlin's sternum, crumbling him prostrate at Chief Easter's brilliantly polished, black patent leather shoes. "No legal parsing here, none of that bullshit. The new Guard is about direct talk. Nothing cynical. Nothing sarcastic. Nothing doubting. We saved your ass. Now shape up! Or take the booking."

Spradlin couldn't breathe until Chief Easter's hands cupped under his arms lifted him loose from the grasping concrete. "Breathe slowly through your nose. Don't try to stand, let me hold you up until your fourth breath. Breathe slowly, more slowly. Do you understand what the new Guard means?"

"Yes," Spradlin lied.

"Good. So ends Lesson One."

2.

But what was the lesson, Spradlin wondered at the time and now? Apparently obedience or at least genuflection toward Chief Easter's ministrations.

"Oh, more new Guard stories," his daughter Ann had said, whenever he started in on recollections.

"Your father's favorite time of his life," his wife Delia said. "He keeps coming back to it like a cat in your lap."

Isn't a cat already in your lap? How do you come back to it?

She didn't understand Chief Easter was not a recollected animal, however lithe and warm. He was the animal's energy and something to pay attention to when suddenly paying attention to nothing no longer dominated your thought. That moment when the outside suddenly blossomed apart from your self-celebration, and careful calibration of your body's wondrous implacability. There were the sweet sand dunes of the New Jersey seashore, scrub pines placed almost perfectly to mark off the horizon, and distant white sparks of surf against the too blue sky. And a leader to follow.

Over the drone of very distant floor buffers Chief Easter's tone washed in from distant seas: "The New Guard won't be easy. We know that. The New Guard challenges a whole lot of what's currently in place, having been set here for hundreds of years. We're the oldest fighting force in the nation's history, and we've been battered and diminished by history and a myriad of random hierarchies beyond our control. But we're still here and more *foundational* than all the other services. Can we develop in new and better elite directions? Can we demonstrate quietly and subtly in ways so compelling that they will, of themselves, elicit followers and allegiances that are so strong as to withstand the torrents of old patterns? Can we do this? Can we find the right tools and more importantly perform in ways that command reverence and attention? Can we inwardly focus so that whatever outward disappointments, setbacks, hostilities, become insignificant? Do we have the inner resources to serve as such wondrous examples we shall compel, actually compel remarkable respect, indeed emulation? We have to build the belfry so sturdy that when we begin to ring, nothing can resist our sound."

"Nothing and nobody," Moulton echoed.

"And it begins interiorly. So that how we carry ourselves, how we dress, how we speak to each other, all become signals of our new excellence."

"Notice how people speak about Chief Easter on this base," Moulton said. "They've already recognized something extraordinary is happening."

Spradlin thought, then and now, was anything really extraordinary happening? Perhaps the only thing extraordinary was his own malleability.

"The New Guard begins inside of you, in the ways you perceive what is going on outside of you. You have to adjust the lens, shift the prism so that reality breaks into new spectrums. That begins with mastering the history of the Guard. But study must parallel actual practice, so we can guide your learning and at the same moment improve your bearing, your stature, your posture within the confines of this very limited place. We'll show you how to move the boundaries simply by standing upright near them. You're floundering and we'll give you spine."

And it was true enough, Spradlin thought, I was floundering. I wanted to be so many things and was nothing. And it seemed Chief Easter was everything. The quiet ramrod competence radiating in widening circles to those around him.

"The New Guard will outlast the old," he said as if telling a secret, "but only if we can bring it to full fruition in my lifetime. The New Guard is restorative, re-invigorating, above all deliberate in its competent action, firm in its commitment. We are here to serve the public and establish the safety of our shores—that's the mission that must be like a light fixed on our foreheads, showing us constantly the way. Before all others we were commissioned by Congress to protect our shores. Before all the others. We are and will be the first line of defense of the homeland. That's a precious charge, precious commitment, precious mission. Only a very few are worthy of it. We'll make you worthy of it. "

The only time he had heard such clear sentiments uttered with such quietude, such sturdy almost automatic near whisper Spradlin thought occurred when that cardiologist explained his prescription note: "You'll take these the rest of your life, twice per day. They will alter the architecture of your heart, reducing the strain and giving you more years than actuaries might predict. I'm sure that is important to you. You take them everyday."

"Take your pills this morning, Dad?" His daughter's daily greeting.

3.

On his first liberty from Sandy Hook he drove south to the alleged best beach in Wildwood, New Jersey. On the boardwalk there he quickly bought khaki Bermuda shorts, flip flops, and T shirt to assume civilian identity, and after almost a dozen Gin and Tonics slumped down, left leg over the fat edge of a faux leather Lawson chair, with cracks in the vinyl, at a USO EM common room a mile back from the sea. Just before noon the next morning Bosunmate Moulton found him and prodded him awake.

"Chief Easter needs you."

"Liberty ends tomorrow at 0800."

"The New Guard needs you now. We have a chance to serve, a chance to demonstrate what we're about., a chance to set the hook into new recruits. Off Portland, they need help effecting a rescue. Lifting a sunken yacht."

"It's not in our district."

"Get up! You little shit! Tell me, please tell me, what's in our district?"

"Okay, you win."

"The New Guard wins. Don't forget it. Live it, and don't forget it."

Part III: At the Falls

In a Guard grey van the three of them drove straight through to Portland despite torrential rains and a canvas rattling wind. In neatly pressed foul weather gear Chief Easter spoke above the slosh hitting the van, "Let the adrenalin flow. You can tell there are times when your example will move the most listless to action, to commitment. We've been promised this mission. The New Guard will not fail. You've locked onto a crucial moment, a liberating moment, so take it, Seaman Spradlin. and let's show all who can see what the New Guard is about." He paused apparently to register something outside through the smeared window, then said, "Times of maximum achievement are always times of maximum risk. That's the supreme sinew of life itself. You simply cannot yank one without yanking the other. Do you understand?"

"Not exactly."

"You'll see as action supersedes thought. When your time comes you'll seize it. I'm very confident of that."

Spradlin thought, *why didn't I see the man spoke with deliberate deception, a calculated, enigmatic rhetoric designed to gather up someone already ripe for followership? I couldn't then believe the emperor was shallow or more likely empty. Perhaps because he wasn't. . ..*

"It's all pretty simple," Easter said, "when we get there, it's likely I'll be the senior non-com on the scene. No officer will be there—it's, after all, a task requiring real expertise, not academy witless training. I'll be senior and defacto in charge and we'll work harder and longer than anyone else on the scene. You understand and believe that don't you? Of course we acknowledge that. I want you to focus on the coming effort. You'll have resources you couldn't believe you possessed. We'll free them for the New Guard. And Bosunmate Moulton is the best handler of a forty-boat in the business. You'll have to be the muscle for this quick operation and you'll need a strong, very strong, stomach. Do you understand?"

"A strong stomach?"

"Yes, what you'll see when we get the yacht up could be nauseating. Doesn't have to be, but could be. But you'll be the oldest of the old salts about it, won't you, Jack?"

He called me, "Jack," not "Seaman Spradlin," not something else. And I was blissful at the commaraderie of that statement.It seemed I was fully taken in. Therein. There-in.

And it was just as he had ordained. Not an officer in sight—just frantic seamen and a flock of third class bosunmates in search of a Chief. Easter slipped quickly into command. He quickly put the three divers on a separate forty-boat, moved the buoy tender into better position to the orange float marking where the sunken yacht had been located. He did a quick calculation and abandoned deep diving equipment, sending two divers down immediately and ordering an immediate assessment. If the Warrant Officer commanding the buoy tender had reservations about taking orders from Chief Easter they were apparently put to rest after a brief conversation. Spradlin could see the Warrant Officer ended up nodding continually, his forearm in Easter's gentle grasp. The deckforce unfurled two weighted manila lines and wound each around the double reel added to the buoy tender's crane.

The divers re-emerged. Easter knelt and conversed quietly with each, he delivered two cable hookups to them as well as a narrow, tough giant sling and sent them to return to the yacht.

"Lay out five body bags," Easter shouted to the forty boat crew. "You will be handling remains and we'll be attentive to the sacredness of that task. Do you understand? These are last remains—their final handling will be sacred. God will bless your work and concern. Do you understand that?" Easter paused, "Do you? I need to hear it!"

"Yes," came in a resounding shout.

"I need to hear it in nautical New Coast Guard terms!" Easter bellowed out as the ropes began pulling taut, sprinkling the sullen dark sea in their straining.

"Aye, aye, Captain!" came the louder answer from the forty-boat crew.

"You may see things you've never before encountered. Deeply disturbing things. Sickening things. But at all times you will be professional and respectful. That is what the Coast Guard means. Professional and respectful."

Part III: At the Falls

There was a peculiar sudden silence as the lines from the crane grew more taut, and indeed tilted the tender toward the sea. The bow of the failed yacht broke slowly through the scummy black sea, and a swiveling searchlight played over the slanted deck revealing a woman's body mostly naked rammed into a large chock on the starboard side. It seemed her leg had been wedged somehow into the chock clamping her body onto the deck. The leg looked broken and greenish/black in the searchlight.

"Hook the deck and pull it closer," Easter said to the two seamen transfixed on the forty-boat. "Heave it over. Do it now! Do it! Haul it in!" His insistence seemed to break their fixation and the yacht came within grasp. "Untangle the woman's leg. Free her body. Gently. That's good. Ease the leg back out. Bring the yacht in closer. Haul the deck in and lift her off. She'll be heavy, water logged, but pliant. You've got to be gentle. Don't let her tear apart. More toward the bow. One get aboard. Now!"

A seaman from the forty boat leapt across onto the slanted deck but slipped and collided with the body, ramming her leg further into the block, busting a gob of flesh off her left thigh.

"Lie prone," Easter commanded. "Lay back, squirm further up the deck. Ease off her. Crank in the other line. Let's get this craft toward level. For God's sake crank her up now." As Easter spoke water gushed from the port holes of the below deck cabin and as the light played back across the resurrected vessel; bodies inside and floating nudged along the portholes. "Free her and hand her over. Jack! Lock on under her arms and pull her across, but don't let her break apart. Firmly, but gently. Good! Good!"

Decades later Spradlin remembered the heft of her, bloated and gaseous but supple as long-cooked spaghetti and utterly lifeless in a way no woman had felt to him. He remembered that slumping vulnerability of her and the way he warmed to Easter's shouted "Good! Jack. Good!"

They pulled four more bodies out of the craft, each one bloated but still pliant, but it was the last one that erased Spradlin's sense of warmth at their accomplishment. It was a little girl, perhaps six years old, he couldn't tell in yellow pajama bottoms and torn green tank top (had she been practicing looking grown-up?) skin still white but strangely wrinkled and apparently flaking—later Easter called it "grave wax" and somewhat unctuously Moulton referred to the substance as "apdoicera" obviously delighting in Spradlin's ignorance of the term. But the girl was not alone. Her chest and face was festooned with crabs and evidently two lobsters. The crabs were nibbling on her eyes and lips, the lobsters had clamped onto her armpits, and were gnawing as if nothing exceptional had moved the body making their delights more laborious. In response the diver, had tossed his mouth piece away and was vomiting noisily into the black, still water. Easter leapt across and using a switched knife began cutting away the crabs, leaving clamped claws in place for the moment. Sighing and seething he slashed the crabs free, tossing them into the water, then prying the claws off the girl's eyes and lips. The knife suddenly turned into an ice pick as Easter destroyed both lobsters, again tossing them into the sea. The diver stopped vomiting and stepped back aboard the forty-boat and said to Spradlin, "Jesus! The man's been there before, hasn't he? So fucking professional. I can't stand it."

"Yeah, he's been there," Moulton echoed. And the three of them watched, transfixed by the quiet mania Easter displayed preserving what remained of the body.

Moulton's heavy arm fell on the diver's shoulder, "It's what the new Guard is all about," he said pushing down hard on what seemed a sure recruit.

4.

Four weeks later Spradlin was not prepared for the follow-up that took place in a second floor office on Governor's Island, District Headquarters.

"Here's what's happening," a slightly pudgy but impressive senior officer addressed Spradlin, alone in the room and looking past the officer to the spectacular view of Manhattan's Battery Place, nine minutes ferry time distance from the island. "Chief Easter and

Bosunmate Moulton have been assigned to riverine duty in Southeast Asia." The officer paused. "They both need overseas and combat duty for their own careers, which incidentally are quite promising for a mustang like Easter."

"Mustang?" Spradlin asked.

"Oh come on, a non-com who manages to take a zillion correspondence courses to get eventually to officer status. You've heard the term."

"I hadn't."

"To be expected of a reserve," the officer commented. "In any event the duty has been assigned. They wanted to offer it also to you."

"They did?"

"Command did. Are you interested?"

"It's a choice?"

"It is."

"Chief Easter was promoting the New Guard—"

"We all have our dreams."

"He's unbelievably competent in rescue and recovery missions."

"We know that. Riverine warfare is perfect for him."

"Perfect?"

"He understands that combat is the quickest route to command. You want to stay E3 all your life?"

"I'd like to talk to Chief Easter about it."

"Not possible. He's on the west coast on his way to ASEAN assignment now. Who knows mid-Pacific by now."

"Isn't that a little precipitous?" Spradlin later thought he heard Moulton pronouncing the term.

"That's the Guard, *precipitous*. You in or out?"

"You can't build the New Guard in Southeast Asia."

"And that's what you want to do? Play the disciple in your reserve unit."

"Possibly—"

"Better to jerk off on your field weekend or weekly poker parties."

Spradlin then and now thought of crabs feasting on the officer's lips and eyes.

"Easter is a very good man, a terrific leader—"

"For a mustang."

"A real model, someone to look up to, someone to *emulate*—" hearing Moulton again.

"So you're out?"

"Entirely."

"One thing about reserves—they're predictable. Dismissed."

Years later he told his daughter, "They sent him to ASEAN because he posed a threat."

"What kind of threat?"

"Maybe the threat of conviction."

"And what is that?"

"Maybe a sentiment that's so deep, so plowing ahead, that it moves everything in front of it, like the sea coming in finding a way around everything on the beach, simply overwhelming anything. Simply plowing ahead relentlessly."

"But the New Guard didn't happen, did it?"

"It surely didn't. Or at least I couldn't advance it even an inch in reserve meetings."

"And what happened to Chief Easter?"

"I haven't the faintest idea."

"So it's an unfinished story."

"Exactly." And Spradlin thought, but when the vase shatters on the marble steps, maybe Chief Easter will be there, picking up the pieces.

9

Nothing in Newark

"Buddy, Buddy," her calling voice is fragile, lilting as if running over flesh ripples like water. Is she in the bath tub? "Buddy, are you there?" Where else could I be? In the very next room, but her sound is like something from a cave, dark and without wind, though wind, New Jersey torrent, spews around the house, rattling the storm windows. Is she forever calling, *Buddy,* and waiting for the portable radio to reply? Or is it only on my visits? "Buddy," comes that soft cry again. She is asleep or I am. We are. Her room is on another level: some four steps, turn, three steps up. On the turn is a yellow throw rug that decades ago yielded up its rubber backing. Like a rag on a polished surface you can go skittering on the turn. I've always imagined myself vaulting out over the bannister, splayed over the piano below, victim of the sliding throw rug. Throw rug, throw. Pitch, heave, off into the dark *National Geographic* night — a full case of them from floor to ceiling at the bottom of the stairs. And if, having been thrown over the bannister and having been tossed or slid off the piano, would I then have been in position i.e., arms whitely turned out like dead fish, eyes askew and glassy, forehead cold, moist and running, in position to catch four tons of pictured geography of the world? Yellow reams of glossy unreality. I never tired of searching them for sagging or firm brown breasts.

The voice was so soft, so comforting—a kind of balm to slow down the thick, dark turning Newark night. How the windows snarled! Yes, she wants me to have the radio—take the portable radio, I think yes, another enormous sacrifice for an ungrateful world. Is it three or four in the morning? Why should I want the portable? Surely she knows that, but to whom else can the offer be made? The bed four-posted, thick but delicately carved posts, clear now in the dark. Their texture was the key. I could not stop my hands from touching them before I went to bed—sharp wood carving, rough and fixed and myriad with etched insets which rubbed in the dark grew rough, rougher. The bedspread, ancient but blinding white, had nubbin reliefs or carvings to answer the posts. And the spread was thick, heavy. Turning over requires determination.

"Buddy." Gentle voice, call on, I think, listening to the sound, placing it beyond the window rattle or the imagined shimmying of the leafless Newark trees—a summons to another spot beyond. Beyond. Mesmerizing sound: *beyond*. Will the portable issue "Beyond the Blue Horizon," with Tony Bennett spiraling out the flat presence of voice vanished-streams? To be wished, she doubtless would have thought or perhaps not. No matter. Her voice is assurance itself. Newark could be full of danger. Who would deny it? But the most savage act slithers away before her, "Buddy." Is there insistence this time? Certain exasperation? Impossible to say. Perhaps she has spoken once, twice at most. Have I been asleep the whole time?

In the hall, on the turn there is, some ten inches from the floor, a night-light glowing like a young hand in the wood-stained baseboard. The voices comes through that puff of light. Generated by it? When I first started visiting her alone, her odd hours and habits were fascinating. I heard the piano after midnight, saw her on the turn of the stairs, an enormous gossamer presence floating by, never tarrying, never moving the rug. Enormous flabby legs through the lightest pink nylon gowns. Springing over the throw rug, thrown up the stairs by it and then the murmuring portable: garbled laughter and static coming down the turn until some hour when I would have, despite myself, fallen asleep.

Part III: At the Falls

    Once, I sopped by because the rain on the New Jersey Turnpike was too thick, too mad to penetrate, which didn't stop those drivers who thrive on the mist of unseen taillights and swallowed windshield wipers. I couldn't take it. Who can continuously go sixty miles an hour into one grey closet after another? I got off the pike, slinked into Newark, beaten. She met me in overalls rolled above her knees, a flannel lumberjack shirt, and voice like bells set in warm water. Her hair was bandanna-ed and she stood behind a stool-mounted hotplate in the center of the kitchen, struck dumb that I was beyond the shaking storm door. We had tuna casserole from the hotplate. She was tired of using the new stove she said. There was no reason to use the hotplate, but then she had not expected company. After the meal we went down to the cellar. She pointed to jars stored during "the last days of Franklin Roosevelt," (It was then the reign of Johnson), peaches, green beans turned a mud color, all in a row along the paneling—soft bluish pine. There was a T.V. in the cellar, but she didn't turn it on. I sat on a wrought-iron and canvas scoop chairs, legs over its oval legs. She sat on the steps and told me what each card of the deck meant in fortune telling: low spades were moderate trouble and if surrounded by hearts, petty jealousies; low clubs brief trips; low diamonds unexpected but modest acquisitions — "Rather like this T.V., Buddy." It had come from P.S. 138 in Newark, the class of '62, a retirement present. "And this," she pointed to a framed certificate "of endurance," she said —thirty-five years in the Newark school system. "Two pounds overweight for each year." And now the jars and the scope chair and me. "You should have called, Buddy."

    "I know," I answered, "I would have drowned if I left the car."

    "I didn't know it was raining."

    "You were fortunate."

    And so we went up to bed. Four steps, turn, three steps up. On the turn a half-hour later, this time in gossamer blue she said, "Buddy, you may have the portable."

    "No thanks, Auntie Bee," I answered watching the posts materialize, "I'm dog tired."

"All right them, Buddy," she said, evident pleasure in her voice, evident relief. "All right."

Then I heard the string of the bathroom light (on her level) pulled, heard the click and then her coming back down the three steps to flick on the nightlight. Then nothing. Nimbus of pale flesh light, puff of illumination, then nothing till at the last moments before easy surrender to the goose feather pillow, the crackled voices and static running together like wire binding up the night, the house, the Newark skyline.

But this was another time. Her voice perhaps was not the same. That time at breakfast she said, "Eighth graders are the worst and the best, Buddy. Mostly the worst. You cannot terrify them. They live on testing terror. You cannot reason with them. Reason is dumb. Ask them. And so how do you get along?"

"Buddy, are you there?" Sweet, sweet voice out-thrashing the wind with its stillness. I could not listen enough to it. I am trying to hear it as it was, I think, but believe it comes differently now. How could it? I prepare to reject the portable as not potable or something. Will it delight her? But such is not to be for the tone has clarified. And the fragility has stretched out beyond contained and precious ingratiation. I begin to feel there is vulnerability in her question. But am I really awake? I sit up, listen again. Nothing beyond the resolute chatter of the storm windows. The posts at the end of the bed order the room into three symmetrical black screens. But the projector has been turned off.

"Buddy!" from the turn of the stairs.

"Yes, Auntie Bee, yes."

"Come here, please. Please!" This followed by a lilting "Ooh."

I've heard that sigh before, I think, a delicious expression of abundance, requisite satiety —as nice as the warmth beneath the sheets now, the heavy close warmth of the stacked heavy bedspread. Who would want to leave such warmth? But the *Ooh* is familiar or I try to make it so. She always visited us for the holidays and after Thanksgiving dinner we all staggered off to the living room. My father in a yellow leather chair and Auntie Bee in the blue wing chair.

No one said anything for a long while. My father dozed and then she would say so familiarly, "Ooh, ooh, ooh," resting her hands on her stomach and pursing her lips slightly — the flesh of her face puckering it seemed. One last "Ooh" and then she too fell asleep. Or just before Christmas she supervised the decoration of the tree, suggesting various length of string for ornaments so that they "filled in the spaces nature forgot." And when that supervision was over—a profound emphasis on placing one strand of tinsel at a time, absolutely no general hurling — when that supervision was over, she asked me to turn out all the light and then upon command to "plug in the tree." In such radiance came another "Ooh." But was it like the one I hear? How I try to make this "Ooh" familiar, but it is not.

Out of the warmth. Feet on the varnish. Like a leap into a November pond. "I'm coming Auntie Bee."

The "Ooh" continues and I am not asleep it seems for on the turn she sitting obscenely, head resting against the wall, left thigh closing off all but a small leakage of the nightlight. The house is shaking in the wind.

"Buddy," she says not lifting her head off the wall. "Buddy, something is wrong. I can't breathe. Ooh." She rocks back, snaps her eyes shut. Squatting in front of her I take hold under armpits, steady her. There is no question that I might lift her, set her on her feet. Her legs are splayed apart, white appendages beneath the blue immense nylon gown.

"Do you want to try and get back to bed?"

She swallows very hard, tilts her chin up and down.

"Okay," I kneel to gather torque. "We have only a few steps."

Suddenly she brings one arm furiously across my forehead, knocking me off my knees back onto the throw rug. I skid toward the steps. She swivels to her right, screams out "Ooh, Ooh" again and throws up. Her swiveling releases the light which brings the smell home—stands of vomitus, red-white matter gushing out of her nose and mouth. She tries to cover it, tries to stop it, merely flops over on her side. I scramble back to my feet. So she flung me out of the way

—generous as always. I vault over her and gather up towels from the bathroom. I put on the overhead light.

"Ooh, I'm so sorry, so sorry, Buddy," she murmurs, eyes turned up and back toward me, her head still on the floor surrounded now by the running remnants. "Ooh, Buddy please forgive me. Ooh, Ooh."

I work the towels around her head, wipe off the side of her cheek.

"Do you want to sit up?"

She shakes her head.

"Should I call a doctor?"

"No. Please don't."

"But something's wrong."

She rolls her lower over her upper lip, sits up, says sharply, "Put me back in bed. Get me up. Try, Buddy, try. And no calling the doctor."

Grasping her again under the armpits, I slowly yank upward. Her legs wobble but she rises, thrust enough to clear her back over one, then two, steps. We rest. I pull again. We clear the last step, but if she cannot walk how will we get to her room? She slumps again. I move around her, go back to the landing and pick up the throw rug. I put it down behind her.

"Auntie Bee, if we can get you on the rug, I can pull you to the bed."

Her head wobbles, trying to look back at me. Evidently no strength left. I simply haul her up on the rug. My hands disappear into the thickness of her armpits. I yank backwards and she begins to move. The rug loosens and suddenly we have momentum. We go pulling and sliding toward her bedroom. There is an awkward moment at the lip into the room, but it only breaks our rush for a second and we arrive at the edge of the bed.

"Do you want to try to get into bed?"

She has slumped forward. I bend further down.

"Auntie Bee? Auntie Bee?" For a long moment in which the windows murmur I think she has simply given out. But she makes a weird guttural, gurgling sound and slowly raises her head.

"The rain," she says slowly.

"It's not raining."

"Yes. Yes, it is," she insists, wobbles forward again.

"Can you stand?"

She turns her head, looks into my eyes and smiles a supreme, helpless smile. I have asked the legless amputee to tap dance or perhaps skate off out of my consciousness.

"Buddy," she says in a rush of words, "you ever have them smile at you and say, 'It just doesn't work. There's no way I can make it work'? It happens first in fractions. You notice it first. Then it's like saying, 'Take this rope and pull the wagon over,' but you hand them nothing. No rope at all. That look, as if to say, 'It's not my fault.' Buddy, well it's not. It's not my fault." While she speaks warm liquid slowly surrounds my bare left foot. The smell of urine.

"Okay. Okay. I'll get you in. Lemme know if it hurts."

I squat own, lock my arms under her arms, around her breasts, and thrust up. I feel the pressure in my legs. One foot squeaks on the floor, but I get her shoulders on the edge of the bed, then bend down quickly, pile my shoulder into her back, lift her legs and thrust up again, rolling over on her stomach. The nylon is sopping with urine. She rises in a half push-up position, turns her head toward me and says loudly enough for all the back rows, "It's not my fault."

"I know that. I'll get you another nightgown."

"Don't. Pull the covers up. No. Wait. Turn me over first. I want to be facing up. Turn me over." She slumps down, exhausted again. She is immense, pliant. I kneel on the edge of the bed, roll her once again, yank her back from going over the side. She is moist and pale and smelly. I bring the covers up to hide it all.

"Buddy," she sighs.

I lean in close.

"Thank you, Buddy. Thank you."

"How do you feel?"

Abruptly she draws her knees up. She opens her eyes wide, as if someone were yanking her lids around behind her brain. She opens her mouth but there is no sound. Then at the very peak of my confusion and fear a faint mewling yowl comes out of her, a continuous tone, mild thread of pain being systematically reeled in by something in the darkness.

"Auntie Bee!" I speak sharply to cut off the tone.

Her eyes wildly whip back and forth in her sockets as if she herself could not snuff out the cry. A kind of frantic plea to pull it out, shut it off. Sweat pours out of her forehead. Then just as suddenly she clamps her mouth closed, puts her knees slowly down, sighs.

"There," she says, "there. I can hold. You see." She opens her eyes, smiles at me. "There I can hold. It will be all right. Buddy?"

"Yes."

"Do me a favor. Get a *National Geographic* and read it to me."

"Auntie Bee, who is your doctor?"

"There is no need to call a doctor. I can hold. Everything is going to be all right. No need to disturb Dr. Antietam tonight. We're going to be fine, aren't we?"

"Yes."

"Good. Now do as you're told. Get the *National Geographic* and read it to me."

"Will you be all right?"

"I am all right."

"Can I leave you long enough to get the *National*—"

"Believe me, Buddy, I have no intention of leaving this bed. No intention whatever. Now get the magazine." She speaks so easily, commandingly that I begin to relax.

I replace the throw rug on the turn, flip on the downstairs light. The first issue is on whaling and the Arizona low country canyons. I put it back, hunt for something more sensual. Tahiti Revisited, Dutch Carnivals, the Bavarian Hills, A visit to Spokane, A Train Ride Through the Canadian Rockies, Michigan's Upper Peninsula, and finally the proper antidote: The Women Divers of Mauritius's Pearl Harvest.

I avoid the rug on the way back up. She is not in bed. Not in the room. I rush back to the bathroom.

"Auntie Bee! Auntie Bee!"

Part III: At the Falls

In answer comes a thud and then harsh scratching sounds from the bedroom. I go back into the room but she is nowhere. Then more scratching from behind the closet door. I open it slowly. She is on the floor of the walk-in closet. The same "Ooh." She is half dressed in a fresh nightgown. I crouch down.

"I smelled so."

"Please, Auntie Bee, it doesn't matter."

"It matters to me."

"Don't worry, please. I thought you said you wouldn't get out—"

"Put me back," she says, "I'm sorry, Buddy, but put me back."

"Can you get up?"

She looks at me as if to say "It's not my fault." I quickly get the throw rug again. The pitch into the bed is easier this time and she doesn't draw her knees up, merely turns on her side.

"I'm all wet," she says.

"You want me to towel you off?"

"No. No. I'm all wet, that's all."

"I got the November issue on Mauritius."

She looks at me carefully, then says softly, "You know I don't give a shit about Mauritius."

"That's what one of them said the last year. Think of it, Buddy. That's what one of them said. It was like that the last years. They were so big. 'Today, class, we will take up decimals.' 'I don't give a shit about decimals.' Where do they learn such language? And they're so big now. So much bigger. Where do they learn it? Let me tell you where," she lifts her head up. "At home, that's where. At home. I can scarcely believe it, but it's what they're exposed to, what they hear all the time. 'Today the predicate nominative.' 'I don't give a shit about the predicate nominative.' Of course they don't. Why should they? Why should they, Buddy?" She slumps.

I wedge a pillow under the left side of her face.

"Those last years," she says into the folds of the pillow, "those last years. I'm so tired. What time is it?"

"About 4:30, I think."

"Don't you know?"

"I can check if you want.""
"Where?"
"The clock is in the kitchen."
"Will you try to get up again?"
She shakes her head.
"You promise?"
She nods.
"It'll take a few minutes."
She nods again. I think momentarily of tying her in, strapping her down, but reject it. I plan to use the kitchen for other purposes than telling time.

"I'll be right back. Now please, please rest."
"Of course," she sighs. "I'm very, very tired."
"Good. I'll be right back up. I'll be right back."

Down the stairs three steps at a time. I grab the phone book off the piano, go directly through the swinging door into the kitchen, nearly topple the hotplate, then finally get the light on. Does Antietam have an answering service? No, indeed. His voice is reedy, sleepy, barely comprehending. I describe and re-describe what has happened.

"Where is she now?" he asks.
"Upstairs in her bedroom."
"That's around that little turn, isn't it?" His voice becomes more coherent.
"Yes."
"Damn it. Well, look. I'm sending an ambulance."
"Can't someone look at her first?"
"Who are you?"
"Her nephew."
"I'm sending an ambulance. Look we don't have time to go into it but—are you her nephew?"
"Yes!"
"Well, let me tell you straight out. It's imperative she be moved to a hospital. Imperative. If she dies while you're there —can I speak frankly?"

"Please."

"Well, if she dies there while you're with her, the legal issues are unbelievable. She's got to go to a hospital. Understand?"

"Dies? Is she going to die?"

"She has diabetes. Had it for years. Does nothing for it. Refuses to do anything for it. I don't know how she passed a school physical. Somebody at the certifying board's a damn homeopath or something. That's just for starters. We're wasting time. You stay with her. I'll send the ambulance. I'll meet her at the hospital. Don't let her drink anything."

"She's going to die?"

"She's got to be moved. Goodbye."

"Buddy," comes a cry, weird and muffled, down the turns of the stairs and through the thick swinging door. "Buddy." Am I only imagining it? Is she standing, holding the portable, cord dangling, and everything will be all right. Am I safe and warm beneath the heavy spread? I race back upstairs. She has been calling.

"Don't leave me like that, Buddy." She says. Slowly she draws her knees up. Her forehead beads sweat again.

"I'm sorry."

"No, I'm sorry to be causing you all this trouble."

"Please Auntie Bee, listen to me. Dr. Antietam—"

"You called him?"

"I had to."

"You stinker!"

"Please."

"You stinker!"

"He says you have to go to the hospital. He's sending an ambulance."

"Ooh, Buddy, I'm so lonely." She puts her hand out.

"I'll be right with you."

"You think you will be, but you won't be. At the end of the year a few them come by to say they'll be back. They couldn't live without you. But you don't see them ever. Once in a while in the halls they sulk at you and turn away nervous and embarrassed. You think you will be."

"I'm not your student. This isn't P.S. 138. You ought to rest."

"Rest period. That was perfect." She draws her knees higher. "Heads on the desk, class. The soft warm lights and the drowsy, drowsy atmosphere. Do you remember, Buddy?"

"Yes."

"Now I shall have a rest period, if I can." She closes her eyes, clenches them shut.

Is it her soft, rippling voice or something else, some other proximity that moves me back, back to Miss Cushing's class and rest period years ago? It is impossible to tell, inevitable to feel. The delicious hum of thirty sleeping heads, under her tall presence, slipping off in a mild perspiration—wet forearm—a certain pulling at the back muscles until sleep seemed too uncomfortable, uncomfortable all the way until her voice awakened us.

But her eyes are so clenched and she opens her mouth again. Comes a long yowl. What can I do? How can I stop it? Almost involuntarily I start to reach to put my hand over her mouth. The mewling starts lower this time. I will not be able to stand it.

"Auntie Bee! What's wrong?" I shout it to summon her back, pull her off the lip of some awful roller-coaster ride. Her eyes flash open, lids spring back, eyeballs rolling back and forth. She starts a vague hacking cough, phlegm piling on itself in her throat. I push both my arms under her pillow and lift up, pull up, make her into a neater, tighter configuration to squeeze the pain and the sound out. There is a momentary hush. She coughs, gags, says in harsh whispers, "I can't hold, Buddy. I can't hold."

"They're coming. It will be all right."

But the yowl grows again, then abruptly stops.

"Respite," she sighs. "Sweet respite. The day goes like that Buddy, doesn't it? One hysterical preparation after another, one task, another, until, until you are about to pop—and the idle, mindless banter of your fellow teachers—drivel to hide consciousness of drivel, isn't it, Buddy? Then respite. Golden respite. You couldn't get to the next day without it. But there's no release from planning. None whatever, is there? Always something to be planned, prepared, given, corrected, returned, revised, re-corrected, returned, forgotten, lost. Burst of respite to spray over the chasm you're falling through, always falling."

"Are you tired?"

"Are you here?"

"Of course. I have hold of you."

"Such confidence, you stinker."

"Please, Auntie Bee."

"No please about it. No please. Finish the work, pass it in. We'll discuss it tomorrow. Sometimes just to stand around them, take up their aroma, their pliancy. That's it, isn't it Buddy? Pliancy is all. He had it wrong, the old fool. Pliancy is all. License to wander through it, that's what makes it worth something, eh? To be like them. Never formed, becoming. Ooh, Ooh." She wipes her forehead, swivels to look at me. "How stupid you look, you stinker."

"Why?"

"I'm not going, you know. They'll never get me to leave here. You know that, don't you? Buddy, don't you?"

"Yes. Sure."

"Easy affirmation. I'm already there in your mind and in theirs, but it won't be so. You'll see. You'll see."

The storm windows shake again and for a moment I feel the house is swaying.

"Come here, Buddy, come here."

"I'm right here, Auntie Bee, right beside you."

"Well, come closer then." When I bend down, she says softly, conspiratorially, "I don't think I can hold."

"You can."

"No. I know my body. I do. You live like I do all your life and you know exactly what the body will do, and what it won't. Do you understand? Don't answer so glibly. You're full of glibness. No substance. Little dreams of where you'll be and no attention to what you are or where. Don't deny it. Why should I lie? Why? No reason. Exactly! No reason whatever. So listen to me. You will. I guarantee it and I know what is going to happen and I know whether or not I can hold. My body is clear in my head. You see that?"

"Yes."

"Then come closer and listen to me."

"What is it?"

But she un-tenses, puts her head back deeper into the pillow, breathes in spurts, her mouth twisted open on one side.

"Auntie Bee," I call softly, right next to her ear. No sounds beyond the Newark air-thrash and low gurgling. "Auntie Bee."

It seems her eyes open momentarily but I cannot be sure. I think about the portable. Should I turn it on? She does not say. I do not hear. Instead, I am aware, acutely aware of the scent of excrement, feces stench, rich and thick from the cup of the bed holding her. The gurgling stops. Even the Newark wind slows. Her eyes, open now have rolled upwards. Her lips appear flaccid, drooping. The breathing has stopped. I bunch the pillow under head, prop her as if to avoid the smell, as if to bunch breath back into her. Her hair smells so clean, feels so soft. With the back of my hand I keep gently pushing at it, testing her response.

In a while I move off the bed and sit on the edge of the top step. I imagine the clatter of entry as attendants rush a chrome and white stretcher around the turn in the stairs. An acned supervisor fresh out of P.S. 141 and his black assistant flipping the awkward padded carrier on high rubber wheels. "They all do it," he says as if to calm me down. "None of 'em can hold it. It's the most natural thing in the world. Believe me I know, and they all do it. Freaks you out the first time, but we get so we can't even smell in this job. You should worry about it."

"She did."

"Yeah, none of 'em like it. Nothing about it to like, I guess."

"Nothing," I answer.

He stares at me skeptically, then fits a stethoscope on, listens to her chest.

"Nothing?" I ask.

He nods. "Nothing."

10

Near Death in Venice

It took a search through my two paperback dictionaries, but at last there it was, the Italian term for what I knew was happening—perfect in its junior high school humorous summonings: *infarto*. Could I stagger out to the courtyard of the 17th century building and cry "Infarto!" and would that bring the faux contessa from the upstairs apartment bounding down the rounded stone steps; or would the Destes call for the emergency ambulance boat? Or would the classmates of my eighth grade memory merely roll off their bus seats in mad laughter at my bowel reference? Was this not the ultimate Italian put down–that I should croak while muttering something I imagined referenced only my own evacuation? More likely I would stagger outside in the 3:30 a.m. chill and bellow the term in a way that was incomprehensible to the locals, who would only turn over and wish the intrusive American could hold his liquor better and pay more attention to conventional hours of celebration.

But agony's elephant had put three of four feet (hooves?) on the tippy board over the bowling ball centered northwest of my sternum. Pressing down. The elephant was slowly cracking his way deep into my left chest; I could feel the ribs snapping off as the ball widened its pathway of pain.

Distraction—yes, distraction first and then deep breathing to will away the pain. I turned on the tiny television in the living room of the ground floor apartment. Jiggling ladies latched to rubber strands that wiggled off the cellulite-on three of the four channels. And on the last one a fellow in shorts on a lawn chair with electrodes strapped to his abs, receiving impulses that sharpened the six pack definition of his flesh and all the while talking on a cell phone. These Italians mocked my own obesity and abdominal flab even as they killed me off in the soft Venetian silence a thousand feet (as the inevitable pigeon flew) from the San Stae boat stop.

I couldn't scream "infarto!" Someone would hurl toilet paper from the apartments surrounding the courtyard. It would be undignified. One ought to die with dignity-wasn't that the standard rap in America? The dignified death. Not moaning "infarto" as overweight ladies swiveled in the damp night of grey television haze. Oh, why "infarto"? And then from some place of memory a calm voice said, "Of course it's the Italian form of "mydocardial infarction"—see, it is familiar, you knew it all along. "Infarction has become 'infarto'" Surely you can accept that. Infarction is the true term, the essence of the experience, and the common overlay in several lands is just some reflection of that reality— "Here, son, it's 'infarto' -no disgrace in that. Be of good cheer. You will cry out and they will answer."

Immediately the pain lessened. But I still went into the kitchen and took two St. Joseph aspirin from a glass bottle I had bought on a lark at the coop store in my campo San Giacamo dell Orio. How long and from where had the aspirin appeared on a back shelf of the tiny store, next to some shampoo mixes? Providential move-a signal, doubtless, that at some level the body already knew the ultimate test was on the evening's horizon. Nonsense, I was only suffering stomach pain referred upwards because I had forgone an evening meal, preferring to drink a full liter bottle of Popelmo, a grapefruit soda, itself I suspected rather old on the shelves since this coop was the only place I had seen it—although I knew it from a stay in Venice three years prior, when the drink was intensely popular. So it was the product of old Popelmo, propelling the pain upward and inward and downward and exploding it interiorly—was that it? I took another aspirin.

Part III: At the Falls

The jiggling ladies gave way to blank patterns and then a news program. The carts of milk went by from a back canal to the coop store, an infernal racket—jiggling bottles and cans on rickety dollies pulled by youngish, smoking Italians. And still the elephant lurched on the wobbling board above my heart. Time to call the university's man in Venice, Fabio. Time to give up the ghost of imagining the problem would pass. Besides in the last hour sweats had given way to chills and breathing was becoming more difficult. Fabio would be asleep but he would know what to do.

"Fabio, something's breaking into my chest, crushing it and I'm having difficulty breathing It's been a few hours and it doesn't go away."

"Eh."

"And sometimes I feel like throwing up."

"Eh."

"Are you awake? I'm kinda of worried. I think I might be having a heart attack."

"Eh."

"A heart attack. Infarto! You get it? Infarto!" I shouted over the noise of a passing grocery dolly just outside the kitchen window.

"Sounds serious." Fabio said in his reassuring, sleepy drawl. "I'll call you right back."

"Thanks. I'm sorry to "

"It'll be okay. Don't worry. Just hang up."

Soon enough the phone rang, and Fabio explained: "The ambulance boat is on the way and I having Mrs. Deste come down and sit with you."

"Sit with me?"

"Yes, just in case you need something. The boat should be there within twenty minutes. She can talk to the crew."

It turned out she could only talk to the crew. Not to me. "I don't do English," she said slowly, eying the apartment carefully. She apparently liked the marble floors, the exposed beams but perhaps was as puzzled as I was by the thick canvas like coverings of two of the main tables in the living room. On top of the white canvas were displays of photographs of people who looked vaguely slavic. Were the owners of the flat Rumanian?

"Parlez vous Francais," Mrs. Deste said slowly again.

"Un peu, " I answered grimmacing as the elephant shifted. That displeasure she mistook for loathing of French I suspected. So we looked at eachother across the 7:40 a.m. light coming from the courtyard. She was wearing a simple print dress, no stockings and slippers. She settled in on the narrow white chair opposite the couch I had settled into. I rubbed my eyes and wondered if she could really be a help. She had a certain maternal fullness and seemed to care that I was distracted and evidently hurting a bit and that was comforting, but I had a vague feeling of embarrassment as we sat watching each other and smiling. Suddenly I was transported to Mrs. Hallowell's dancing school for eighth graders and I saw that she wondered if I would, indeed, ask her to dance the newly learned Fox Trot. She was dumpy and unsolicited by the other, bolder fellows and I felt sorry for her. Here I was the last expiring cripple left to reach across the gleaming parquet floors as Mrs. Hallowell said, "Now go to your partner and commence when you hear froggy," Froggy was a metalic clicker with which Mrs. Hallowell liked to begin, end and silence the dances.

Froggy was beginning to click furiously inside my chest. Mrs. Deste dropped her eyes and then asked, painfully slowly: "Two bathrooms?"

She did know some English. Did she want to use the bathroom, or was she finding out about the real estate?

I said "Yes," tentatively, as if to elicit more information.

But there came a wondrous wooden clattering in the courtyard. The ambulance personnel had arrived. All four of them, in orange vests. A large blonde woman banged on the front door. Mrs. Deste let them in. The blonde woman signaled I should not get off the couch. She pushed aside the slavic photographs on the coffee table and her assistant, an elderly fellow with about four days growth of grey flecked beard put a large stainless steel box on the cloth.

Part III: At the Falls

He began attaching electrodes to my arms and chest. The burly fellow behind him explained, "He's going to check to see if you're having a heart attack." The English was clear unaccented.

I thought, what part of Buffalo are you from, but didn't say anything. The elephant had snapped another rib.

Needles on the box moved about and the elderly fellow attached more electrodes to my legs, yanking up on the pajama bottoms. The blonde forced my shoulders back against the couch.

After a few moments of looking at the dials and watching the needles flourish, the elderly fellow said something in Italian and the massive assistant translated. "He says you're probably not having a heart attack, but he thinks you should go to the hospital anyway, since the battery is low and maybe this machine isn't reliable."

"Okay, let me get a sweater."

"Don't get up, she'll get it for you. Where is it?"

"Back bedroom."

Mrs. Deste bounded off the couch and disappeared down the hallway. After a few minutes she came back with my green shawl collar sweater.

"We'll put you in the chair now." the burly fellow said.

"Chair?"

"Outside, in the courtyard," he seized my underarms and directed me toward the door. And there in the tiny courtyard stood a high backed, entirely wooden, including the wheels, configuration that looked like a steroid- distorted wheel barrow.

"In that? " I said.

"Yes, exactly."

I turned and relaxed down on to the wooden seat and suddenly Mrs. Deste began a quick pointed conversation in Italian with the burly fellow, who continued talking to her as he eased behind the chair and tilted me upwards. Mrs. Deste still asking a series of questions apparently, stepped backward on to the marble entrance to my apartment. My rising knees in the wooden chair framed her nicely as I was pulled backwards over the irregular stones of the courtyard.

The burly fellow, breathing a bit from the burden he was pulling, said, "She wants to know what do you pay for the apartment?"

"The university pays. I don't know what the rent is." I replied exasperated at this most Venetian moment.

"I told her about 4 million lira. I'd bet about 4 million lira at least–what do you think of that?"

"When I first came to Venice I used to stay at a pensione on the Lido, cheap–sixty bucks a night for a red metal cot in a narrow room with a bath on the first floor–floor to ceiling windows wide open to the alley way. "

"Good price," the burly fellow said.

"That's not the point. The point is I got to know the concierge pretty well and he said the trouble with Venice was its greed. He'd read me stuff from the daily newspaper about how each day a new record was set by a restaurant someplace in Venice charging for a meal. Something like 650 dollars for a lunch for two visiting Japanese. 'See, that's what will ruin Venice–that desire to gouge foreigners'"

"Maybe 4 million is too much for a first floor in this campo. It's way off the tourist trail, you know."

We had reached the first formidable obstacle—a bridge requiring ascent of five steps and descent of seven. Evidently they had found a back way in, away from San Stae, a side canal I hadn't ever seen before. The burly fellow grasped his side of the chair and the elderly attendant and the blonde took the other side, but clearly they were having trouble lifting the apparatus with me in it.

I got out of the seat, walked over the bridge. They carried the chair after me and then insisted I get back in. And I thought, if I can walk up over the bridge and down, perhaps I'm not really having a heart attack. Maybe it was the Popelmo. Maybe the hospital trip was truly unnecessary. On the other hand the pain had not really subsided. Some internal warning mechanism insisted that first I'd waited too long to call Fabio and now I could not compound the error by dismissing these realtor/saviors who had come to bear me away in a wheel barrow.

Part III: At the Falls

Venice in the early morning is ravishing—the canals are silent and creaseless, dark enamel sheets of slick, motionless sea, reflecting the myriad pastels of the lining palaces and buildings. The air is moist cool. Everything is shuttered; life suspended. The Grand Canal empty save for one distant, utterly noiseless vaporetto about to turn the corner of the reverse S shape. The ambulance boat moved in a stately muffled fashion. (At the hospital when we got there, Fabio's sister, his designee of reception, said "We were hopeful that they came in so slowly and without sirens. You must be okay.") There was an inviting cot on the boat with a thick white swaddled mattress and I imagined it would be a pleasant way to exit Venice, so stretched out, watching the tops of the palaces and the silken soft blue sky, muttering with the executed prisoners, "Ah ciao Venezia bellisima." A little trip to the Ospidale Civile, then exit to your appointed 12 year term of interment on San Michele Island before final disposal to the lagoon's engulfing waters (300 square miles or so), but nobody suggested I switch from the wooden chair to the comfortable cot. We turned off the Grand Canal and went to the outside, in view of San Michele itself. Was it significant to be given such a slow tour of Saint Michael's cemetery island before docking at the hospital?

There was a furious clattering of wooden wheels on ancient stones from the dock to the hospital's reception area and then I was tossed onto a full gurney, rolled into a separate waiting room and then attached again more fully to electrodes. Two youngish interns in green short sleeves leaned in and after checking the monitors said. "You are having a heart attack and we give drugs to end it."

"So the other machine was wrong?"

"Yes. But it's okay. There is still time."

Still time, I thought. It's close then? What is it? The catastrophic slipping away? The big sleep? A rushing overflight direct to San Michele? There had been sea gulls on some of the gravestones—stiffly standing seagulls enjoying the still morning air, and meticulously maintained short straight narrow pine trees around the edges of the field of monuments.

"I am Roberto," one of the attendants said to me, leaning in over my head. "The drugs are going in now."

"I'm feeling better," I answered. "The chest pain has stopped."

"Of course," Roberto answered, "the drugs are working already."

"I felt better on the boat, too, without the drugs."

"Of course," he answered, strapping down my wrists.

The dismissive tone worried me momentarily, as if he were steeling himself for my departure–one more corpse to be certified and disposed of, was that it? The gurney moved across cobblestones, onto smoother marble into an elevator. I tugged on the wrist straps which seemed to come undone, or at least I felt in the lifting up of the elevator that I had come loose from the bed, collapsed somehow upwardly, detached and dropping somewhere into a void that wasn't clear at all. From the shrouding darkness, the collapsing dropping I received a warm rush of welcome–a really exciting dizzying feeling that whatever was happening was both inevitable and quite pleasant. Positively sweet. So this is it, and it's not so bad. In fact it's quite wondrous and enveloping and magically caressing and sweet, soft and sweet and full of pillows of pleasantness. What could it be turning me softly around and around, bearing my weight up under the arms and under my legs and lowering me into some sweetly damp, soft place. Wow I thought, if this is death, bring it on. There's nothing here but sweet release. No need to worry about not seeing wife or children–they'd be fine, especially if I could convey to them the sweet exquisiteness of this experience. Come follow me.

And even as I wallowed in this weird bliss I sensed a certain pulling away, disassociation from the joy, watching myself experience the thrill of the soft touchingness. And that disassociated watching plunged me back into two other moments of near expiration. One in my 17th year. I lived that summer in a shack erected on the mammoth telephone poles of the salmon trap that was floating 1000 feet out in Clarence Straits some twenty miles from Ketchikan, Alaska. The A & P corporation had implemented a plan to prevent illegal pouching of Salmon from its traps by posting one seasoned trapper and one naive college student in a shack on each trap. It was our job to prevent pirate ships from ripping off the catch (Salmon swam along the shore, turned against the chicken-wire wall that connected the trap to the shore, moved along the wire into the trap and then were turned through a series of net openings into the final spiller area the bottom of which was a net that the company ship could pull up once per day to off load the fish).

There was nothing to do on the trap all day but read, fish, sleep, cook elaborate meals over a coal stove in the ten foot square shack. A & P did give us –my experienced trapper roommate, Frank, was a local from Ketchikan who had come to Alaska, as had all white settlers before statehood for reasons no one ever was so stupid as to inquire about– a small boat and two oars. Frank had brought along a five horse power motor, so whenever the rain stopped Frank and I explored the straits and visited the traps anchored off the myriad islands. The nearest trap to us belonged to a single trapper named Oscar–it was about a ten minute run further out the straits. I envied Oscar his no trapmate status, alone with his 50,000 salmon awaiting their canning in Ketchikan. But it became clear over the summer that being alone on a trap, indeed living alone in Ketchikan during non-fishing season had put Oscar more than a little beyond the norm. He had a peculiar twitch and throat stroking motion and a wheezing jovial delivery as his eyes looked beyond you to some apparition apparently closing in. "We'll keep Oscar from getting too dingy," Frank always said as a prelude to setting out up the straits.

It occurred to me Frank himself was "dingy." At night he always chewed a local root, as he called it, and when I asked whether it might not be habit-forming, Frank answered easily, "Nah, I've been chewing it for twenty years." He'd lived for over three decades in Ketchikan, working the traps in the summer and resting through the long winters–sometimes working at the canneries, but more likely sitting at one of Ketchikan's 43 bars (in a town of less than 5,000 people). The only women available were so called "cluetches"–dysfunctional Blackfeet Indian women who worked the bars as companions/prostitutes. Frank kept a large collie dog at his home in town and told me matter of factly, "I'd as soon throw a fuck into my lassie as fool around with them cleutches" Sometimes sports fishermen came to tie off the trap and fish for salmon still outside the wireworks. Mostly they were Aleutians, short dark skinned fellows, about as taciturn as could be imagined, but smiling and tireless in hauling in catch after catch.

The water temperature of Clarence Straits was about 42 degrees–"It'll kill you," Frank said, "in about ten twelve minutes if you don't get out. So remember that."

When Frank and Oscar talked it was monosyllabic and apparently restricted by my presence–later I would come to understand Frank was probably lamenting the stupidity of his trap-mate who did not understand that the fish catch could be sold off to pirate captains for a handsome 200 dollars per thousand. A & P had bet correctly on my ignorance or morality. But at the time I only understood that I was extraneous and a drag on the society of the two trappers. So I began walking the trap, which in fact was about the size of two football fields. On quiet days the cabled telephone poles that hung the chicken wire dried out in the sun and with regular boots you could walk along the poles until you were well over a hundred yards from the shack. On sunlit days you could see thousands of herring in the trap–with the salmon that had swum along the lead and entered the cages all the way to the spiller. And the algae that grew along the wire mesh convinced them there were in a walled cage. Only the terror of the spiller net moving them upwards toward delivery to the brailing ship prompted them to test the algae "wall" and they discovered they could slip through the wire spaces. They could nose through the blockage and get outside the trap, since they were so much smaller than the salmon.

So I walked slowly out along the vast poles holding the trap together, finally reaching the lead connection to the shore the furthest point from the shack. But at the lead some of the logs had been tilted down a bit and were perpetually wet, covered with a green very slippery slime. And I lost my footing. My right foot splayed outward over the side of the log and I pitched forward smashing into the top of pole and tried to latch on to it as I slid to the right toward the quiet, unlapping waters of the straits. I tried to embrace the log as I swiveled to the right into the water. My arms hugged the green slime and didn't hold and I rolled kicking free of the log. The sea was like an unbelievable snake that simply took hold of me and throttled me in its chill grasp, forcing the air out of my lungs and stunning my body in its ice grip. Instinctively I called out to Frank and Oscar, but quickly realized they couldn't hear me at such distance. The shack had no windows, just a gun slat on each side (residue from the 1930s when allegedly the trapwatchmen actually used gunfire to hold off pirate ships–hence the exorbitant pay the union demanded for trapwatchmen). Frank and Oscar would be talking in the shack with walls thick enough to stop 30–06 slugs. Drinking coffee and laughing while I drowned.

I would have to get back up on the log on my own. No sense shouting and losing what little energy the water had not already drained away. And I drifted off from myself, imagined the struggling creature with perhaps only nine minutes left to solve this interesting problem. Eventually the snake released a bit–the cold was not so hostile, perhaps actually more welcoming. Still. I could try to get back up on top of the log. Kicking against the sea I flung two arms over the top of the log and clamped down with my fingers but the slime merely eased them back toward the water as I fell away backwards again. And the spiraling consciousness above the scene noted, so that was one attempt–there would be enough left for perhaps two more. And if both failed to secure a hold, why then Clarence Straits would win and the coldness might turn into some eternal warmth. So let's slide along the log a bit and feel for a hand hold. But there was none. My arms ached, almost felt unsocketed in their slow flail along the pole.

And then my left hand felt an indentation in the log, yes, there was a sunken cable strapping the pole to a cross log underneath somewhere, too deep to find a foot hold under water, but enough of an indentation for some fingers to clamp on to its metal sides free of slime. If I could put fingers from both hands on the edges of the indented cable maybe there would be enough heft to swing a leg up onto the log. Then maybe a heel could be socked through the slime deep enough to leverage the rest of my body up. Yes, there was one last chance the spiraling above presence recorded in a mocking whisper–why not give it a spin? The alternative was looming pleasantly enough–expiration, even near-expiration, released its own endorphins. I remembered runners apparently "hit the wall" when the body signaled—I give up. Death do your worst. And I was aware that whatever the worst was, it was not unwanted or unalloyed fear–it was something else, a dropping away that was not in the least worrisome. It was in the very broadest and most smiling sense, "okay." So try one more time and if for some reason it doesn't work, why then the payoff was particularly and surprisingly acceptable. Sweet surrender to a swell watery grip that announced pure stop-time and pleasant surcease from trying, from any inclination to try. I squeezed fingers, flailed a leg, dug a heel into the log, felt it bite, hoisted the soaking body upwards. And heard not Frank or Oscar but Roberto hollering, and hollering:

"Mr. John, Are you there? Mr. John are you there? Can you hear me? Lift your legs. Mr. John, are you there?" The bed was collapsing inwardly as they furiously cranked my legs above my head.

"Mr. John, can you hear me?"

"Yes, I can hear you."

"Good. Keep your legs up. Blood pressure is returning. Returning."

Returning indeed but the spiraled-presence nodded and indicated the option of another avenue would be renewed and renewable in tandem with each choice to hoist oneself from the cold, welcoming sea. Roberto said, "I knew we had not lost you. I knew that."

2.

I was in a different room–there was a mammoth stainless steel door with a porthole window. The door slid back and forth and Roberto eased it shut. I was aware of buzzing machinery overhead and electrodes all over my body. The bed was being cranked flat again, having furiously collapsed to get my legs up, my head down. The top of the trap log felt wet, cold, slippery all right, but I was out of the water and it would be easy enough to pick my way carefully back to the shack.

"Fell in, eh?" Frank said when I came through the door, and returned to his confab with Oscar.

Oscar got me a blanket. Roberto tossed a towel like light blanket over me on the bed.

The Aleutians came in the early morning, anchored off the trap and fished all day and half the night. They never asked for water, for food. They never took a break. With lanterns ablaze they untied after 10:30 p.m., and were gone. I watched one of them catch 154 King salmon in one sixteen hour period. Each salmon weighed, I figured at least 10 pounds. The apparently trapped herring inside the chicken wire and attracted salmon lucky enough to have avoided the trap lead.

Neither the Aleutians nor Roberto spoke much English. Roberto handed me a plastic pitcher and said–"Pee here. No out of bed." Then he was gone. He slid the hefty door back along the side wall. It glided almost noiselessly. The whole room was painted an iridescent sky blue. The grey linoleum floor sparkled from some flecks of mica apparently embedded in the tiles. I was alone in the room, but over the door was a television camera and I could see through the open door to the nurses' station where there was a bank of monitors. I assumed my bed appeared on one of them.

Suddenly Roberto was back at the door. "Dr. Risica will see you in about two hours," he said and turned away. My right arm was still strapped down to the bed and the drip of something steadily descended into the back of my hand. My fingers had been torn by the rusted wire cable around the distant log, and water slopped over my face as I rested on the pole, delighted that I had gotten free of the chill sea.

"I thought I was dropping, dropping away," I said to Roberto who was no longer in the room. The steel door had its own distinctive gleam and coldness, like some meat slicer intersecting the iridescent blue. Why couldn't I lift my arm? The extreme pain was gone in my chest, but things weren't normal. Residual pain, a kind of mild ache as if the elephant had really stretched my rib cage in some weird way. At the same time I had a certain longing, a nostalgia for the pleasantness of the dropping away. I was anxious to get back there–the disassociated thrill of thinking–say, this isn't too bad. You've been told a lot of hooey about the end of life and here it is and it's not bad at all. It's swell in fact, sweet and swell and worth hurrying toward.

Later when I was back in the states a colleague wondered with mounting excitement, "Were you in the alleged tunnel. Was that it? Were you really in the tunnel with the white light at the end and the warm feeling and the bath of illumination and the all-powerful longing to merge with the light?"

"Not really, but it was pleasant, very pleasant and I wanted it to go on very long time. I didn't want it to stop."

"You were in the tunnel."

"There was no tunnel–only the black and chilly Clarence Straits and the smiling Aleutians."

"And the cleutches–let's not forget the 'cleutches.' They were there to make you happy. Keep you quiet and happy, contented, exhausted."

The water on the log top was much warmer, shallower, sun-filled. So warm you wanted to drink it, celebrate it as the substance it was, not the lethal agent it could have been. I remembered if you wanted to fish off the edge of the trap and needed bait, the standard chore was to throw a line of triple hooks so that they sunk through the milling school of herring and then you simply yanked up. Because the herring were so bunched up they couldn't get out of the way in time and, presto, you had four or five herring hooked and loadable to your pail for bait. Once, I had let the hooks go too deep and they had drifted to the side against the kelped chicken-wire. They snagged up some ten feet down and I decided, against all reason, to jump in to break them free. I had Frank wet me down first, but when I jumped it, the coldness still grappled me like the snake of termination, expelling all my air, leaving me shivering and gasping as I sank along the wire, frantic to free the triple hooks. It took three plunges to get all the hooks loose. And at the end I understood perfectly how you could die after ten minutes in the water.

And what would happen now? Oscar said, "You sit by the stove in your blanket and in forty minutes you dry out. Then you go back with Frank to your trap. You're lucky, you are."

"Dr. Risica will tell you what's next, but he won't come in until tomorrow." Roberto said.

"Didn't you say he'd come in two hours?"

"No. He won't. He'll come tomorrow."

"And in the meantime I wait here, inert, I suppose, and pee in this plastic bottle or whatever."

Roberto nodded, not following my hurried speaking, then unstrapped my right wrist, freeing me completely.

"No getting out of bed."

"If I need to pee. . ."

"In bed. Use that" Roberto pointed to the plastic pitcher.

At 17 I suppose confrontation with death is not really conscious or possible. You spend most of your time figuring how to extricate yourself from the hemorrhaging situation–and there is a calmness to your faith that you will find an exit, a path back onto the log. It's merely a matter of leverage and agile muscular power, of which there's a plenty. You need only find the opening and then celebrate the nimble departure. Wrap in the blanket and dry out. Lie on the crisp muslin of the Italian sheets, listen to the clicking machine overhead, stare at the television camera and take in the gorgeous blue sunlit sky through the narrow line of long windows, on their sides, at the ceiling. Noiseless Venetian water light reflecting off the ceiling. And sleep.

Fabio woke me up. He came in with two green suited residents. The three of them, each powerfully built stood at the end of my bed and talked animatedly in Italian. Were they discussing my condition or were they debating the relative merits of spritz bars near the hospital? Then Fabio said in English "They want to know if you are having any chest pain. Are you?"

"A little. Some, here," I pointed to the left side of my chest.

Near Death in Venice

More animated discussion in Italian. Evidently the wrong answer.

"What's going on?" I asked Fabio.

"They think you only had a very mild attack. They think you'll go home soon. Maybe after they ask you to ride a bicycle or something to see if you're okay."

"So that's good news."

"Yes, but Dr. Risica will make the judgment and he'll come later today or maybe tomorrow, they're not sure."

"They think it wasn't so bad?"

"Yes. No so bad at all. You'll be going home pretty soon. They're pretty sure of that. One of them used to eat at my father's restaurant."

"Is that a good sign or a bad sign?"

Fabio didn't laugh, instead he said, "Depends on the time they came in. You just rest today and tomorrow Dr. Risica will tell you what the plan is. I'll come back tonight. You can use this cell phone to call home."

"To the U.S.?"

"It should work–give it try later today. Don't let them see you with it. You're not supposed to use cell phones around this equipment, but they don't really care. They'll start feeding you this evening. Just rest, relax. I'll bring you something to read tonight. Just sleep. Don't worry about the projects. I'll keep them going."

"I noticed there was no computer printout in the ambulance boat."

Fabio said, "I know. I know. They didn't adopt the program." He smiled. "We borrowed most of it anyway."

Three years before Fabio and I had advised a project providing the ambulance services of Venice with a digitized map of all the canals, with bridge heights, water levels, tides and canal depths figured in. Ideally the program could take any two addresses and plot the fastest canal route between the two sites. All the boat captain needed to do was punch in the two addresses and a map highlighting the routing would print out, so that even the most novice navigator could go directly and swiftly to the scene of the emergency. It was precisely the sort of computer program that set Fabio salivating. Here he was the apostle of Venetian history–After a few spritzes he'd look at me with the shimmering outside sea toward Murano as a backdrop and say slowly, turning the syllables over lovingly, "There have been in all of history about only 3 million Venetians"–this worshipful past-master– in deeper love with computer technology than any of the Titians or Tintorettos he strolled among each day. It was a joke at the university that any of us who dealt with the Venice Project center could send Fabio a remark about the latest gadget and get back immediately a detailed appreciative response, followed by a purchase order request. Sometimes I contemplated telling him I had an advance prototype of a Pentium 12 chip, was he interested?

Three years ago Fabio spent an hour showing me software that no only reproduced the footprints of buildings in New York, but each floor in comparison to other floors of other buildings on the same plane throughout Manhattan. His enthusiasm increased as the cursor leapt from building to building on the screen. From the late 1980s he had set our university's students to digitizing the maps of Venice, so precise that the canals could be measured on the screen–not only the canals, but the bridges and calli or roadways, not only those but the steps to the bridges, the steps of the docks. He had assembled the largest data base of Venice's totality in the history of the world. A CD of all the flagstaff holders, all the belfries, all the outdoor art, all the well-heads, all the churches, all the museums, all the ceiling paintings. He dreamed of creating substantial stalls of computers into which patrons like porn fanatics could step, pull curtains and call up the floor plans of the Doge's palace or San Rocco, click on the walls, zoom in on the paintings, zoom further in on the parts of deterioration, click for the cost estimate restoration and then switch further to the roof tiles or the nearby boatdocks, or the furthest reaches of the lagoon for a GPS survey of wetlands and marsh growth, all the abandoned hunting lodges in the lagoon. The ultimate Venice in a box.

The ambulance boat computer mapping project turned out to be a bust, with the coup de grace delivered by the least computer literate student in the project team–the ultimate outcast, a stout fellow named Max, who specialized in human rather than software relationships. The other three members constantly railed against Max because he never kept his part of the software system operative–he failed to enter his data on bridge heights, he never helped with the complex algorithm that factored in tide charts and schedules, he ignored data on canal depths or sludge deposits. He drank spritzes and endlessly socialized with local Venetians, and then spent lavish amounts of money taking his friends to his parents home in Prague. He never did any of the reports or tasks assigned to him by the project team, by Fabio or me. Instead he took the ambulance drivers out for spritzes, and endless bottles of Veneto red wine. And in the last week of the project he discovered what none of the computer jocks were able to find: in fact maps were totally unnecessary, useless. There were only three basic routes an ambulance could follow getting around Venice–up the grand canal, around the backside, or through the Rio di Ca' Foscari. From those three routes it only required a driver pick one canal spur and go as far as possible then off load the wooden rolling chair. It was a calculation any Venetian could make automatically, or any outsider with about two hours orientation to. Within those water routes Venice was so compact as to be walkable in a few minutes. Venetians understood that if you came in from the train station the walk to San Marco at the other end of the city was far faster than taking a local vaporetto down the Grand Canal. Walking would cut the time in half. It did not sit well with his partners that Max disproved the very basis of the project.

"I didn't recognize the driver," I said to Fabio who seemed unhappy at the reminder of our technological failure.

"I think they change drivers often," he answered.

"Think of the time those kids spent getting the program to work."

Fabio was uninterested. Venice was about, he told me one afternoon as we munched trapanzini sandwiches near the project center office, Venice was about future technology. It has always been at the cutting edge and would have to be again to regain its old stature. It could not become, he would not let it become, a theme park empty in the later evening, void of daily life. But he knew the city had been shedding population since World War II, down from 140,000 to barely over 60,000 in 2004. "In the old days, the Venetians tagged every single tree growing in the Veneto so they would have a supply of ship's masts when the need arose. Even now the Veneto region leads all of Europe in computerization of business possibilities. You can read about it in *The Economist*."

"There wasn't even a printer in the boat. That would have been nice," I said.

"Stupid, but nice," Fabio said.

"Maybe it was just the Popelmo I drank last night. Maybe I didn't have an attack."

Fabio turned to the residents and there followed a long discussion in Italian before Fabio turned back to me: "They say it would have been too dangerous to use the drugs they used if you didn't have heart attack. So you definitely had one, maybe still are having it. Dr. Risica will decide."

I could tell Fabio recognized my disappointment. "But they think it was a mild attack," he added.

3.

On Saturday morning, Dr. Risica appeared flanked by four residents. He wore dark green tight trousers, a longish white untucked shirt and slender suede shoes that seemed so conformed to his feet as to be climbing gear. He seemed astoundingly fit, narrow, lithe and with a deep bass voice. I immediately I sensed he was the savior I longed for, before even I understood my longing.

"Are you having chest pain, still?" he asked resonantly.

"Yes, but it's very slight, mostly here," I clamped my right fist over my left chest.

"And on a scale of one to ten it's what?"

"Four, probably only three or slightly less."

"We have stopped the attack, but we need to look and see the extent of the damage. We must do an angiogram, maybe angioplasty, maybe some stints."

Three new terms. "Angiogram?"

"Dye through an artery–we can watch on a screen how the blood flows. If plasty is required we expand the vessel, widen it and if that doesn't work we insert a metal coil to hold the blood line open. You are awake the whole time. About forty minutes. Do you understand?"

"When do you do it?"

"Monday morning."

"Pain?"

"Some. Not much. Discomfort more than pain."

"The coil. . ."

"Stint," Risica corrected me.

"How long does it last?"

"If it lasts through the first six months, it will last a long time–years. The first months are critical."

"Why?"

"The body sometimes rejects the stint, tries to clog it over. Then we're-stint' it. That's quick and easy. We'll do it first thing Monday morning. You just rest, let the drugs keep everything open."

"It's boring."

"What isn't? Monday will come quickly." Risica turned away and motioned to his minions.

I recognized the stout one from yesterday's meeting with Fabio. And the fellow more than acknowledged me. He said, "Tonio will prep you tomorrow afternoon."

"He'll shave you, "Risica elaborated. "A very complete shave. Everywhere we need to cut." He slid the door back and was gone.

I liked the crisp confidence—we'll get to the heart of this problem and excise it. The certitude of surgeons boils out of them in inexorable waves. They squeeze out the fear. And then are gone. The backwash is formidable. Anxiety seems to draw strength for being pushed to the periphery. The great man is absent till Monday–the weekend is all mine, said trepidation. I could feel myself blending back into the muslin, relaxing into a somewhat distant terror. The pain had lessened. Surgeons always like to cut. Perhaps it was only necessary to pick oneself up and exit the premises, catch a vaporetto back to San Stae and be sure not to drink any more Popelmo. On the other hand the blue and reflected light, the shinning sliding stainless steel, the curious porthole window, the glistening pseudo-marble floor, the crisp sheets, and the droning endlessly recording machinery seemed hospitable–a Venice such as must have appeared to Arab traders in the 14th century–way ahead of its time–the crystalline future revealed, dazzling in its soft declaration of the human possibility. See we can make a city of innovation amid a muddy swamp–where no one dreamed anything could be built, we built what no one could have imagined. We set the rules to free the imagination, direct it in ways that limited structures in order to intensify them. Perhaps I'd been talking too long with Fabio who perfectly believed that Venice was only about the future, never the past. The decaying foundations, the crumbling docks, the dwindling population, the eroding canals were nothing compared to the dreams Venice engendered–human will was everything, the Venetian noted in passing as he marked each tree in the Veneto a potential ship's mast sixty years from now. His grandson could do the cutting, oversee the long slide to the Arsenal ship building docks. Why not lie on the stiff sheets and soak in the blueness? And I fell asleep.

Once again Fabio awoke me. "I've brought you a literary guide to Venice," he said.

I had hoped for a bible.

"Just clips from writings about Venice," he continued. "Some of them are terrific."

"You ever read *Venice Rediscovered*? " I asked.

"No."

"It will convince you anyone who ever wrote about Venice was lunatic, or perverse or both."

"Maybe the drugs are thinning your brain." He smiled.

Time to change the subject. Nothing of Venice could be lunatic or perverse, unless of course it was done in some advanced way.

"The phone you gave me won't let you call internationally."

"Really?"

"Yes, really. I'm assuming someone in the main office informed Alice."

"Yes, Natalie talked to her, but she had to go to Boston to pick up your son and his bass, is that it?"

"Did she say she'd come over?"

"I don't know."

"Max is supposed to go on to Cuba for another concert—"

"Wait a minute. I can solve the telephone problem, I think. It's the chip. My phone has the proper chip for international calls. I can substitute my chip for yours. It'll work I'm pretty sure."

This technological fix suddenly took hold of Fabio. He produced a small screwdriver and busily set about disassembling his cell phone, then mine. In a trice he switched the chips and reassembled the units. "Try it." he smiled.

"I don't like to be too obvious about using these–we're not supposed to."

"They think they upset the monitoring machinery, but I don't think they really can."

"When I tried using the phone this afternoon, the old woman in the next room started screaming."

"Really? That's fascinating. Give it a try now."

"You want to hear her scream again."

"Sure," Fabio smiled. "Venetians enjoyed the inquisition."

"You're sick."

"Go ahead try it. It's only 2 p.m. in the states."

"If she screams. . .."

"It's only her monitoring equipment, how can she scream?"

"I heard her."

"I'll take responsibility," Fabio said.

I dialed the states and, miracle of miracles, Alice picked up. (No sound came from the adjacent room–was the old woman sleeping?) Alice and I explored the ironies of our careful planning. She and our youngest, Laura, were to arrive in Venice in ten days to finish up the project term with me. Our daughter Emily was to come in from Kazakhstan (where she was a Peace Corps worker) nine days hence. Max was to fly over after a concert. Then in two weeks an old high school friend and her husband were to join us. It had all been perfectly timed. And now the inconvenience of this little event threatened everything. Since I was coherent and feeling okay we decided to let original plans and reservations stand. She would not come over since Max had to be delivered with the coffin like bass air cargo to Logan in two days anyway. Emily would be the first to arrive to check on me.

What I didn't discuss was my feeling that perhaps the angioplasty wasn't necessary–maybe I could just walk away from everything recover quietly in the expensive apartment at San Giacomo Dell Orio. There was no need to commit to a procedure if I could get someone to agree it wasn't necessary. Alice had already been in contact with our usual physician, who though on vacation in Pennsylvania, said to call him on his cell phone. Perhaps he would save me from arterial slithering, tubes within tubes scampering up from my groin into the center of my heart. It was not much of a hope–physician was another word for intervention. One co-sponsored the other.

"You can switch chips," Fabio said, delighted. "I figured you could, but I've never actually tried it. But it works perfectly."

The transposability of technology thrilled him, predictably enough. He was determined that data collection and storage on Venice would eventually transform his city. That he could triumph over geography and get the overweight American in touch with his family, simply by using a screwdriver and native ingenuity was further evidence of the viability of his Venetian dreams.

In fact the whole Veneto was better wired than almost any place with the possible exception of Sydney Australia, he had told once over spritzes on a hot late July afternoon.

Since he was ecstatic about his small transistor switch performance, I decided to risk a further request.

"Do you think it might be possible to postpone the angioplasty?"

"So Alice could get here?"

"Possibly," I answered, conscious that there would not be such a chance. I realized her intended visit would be the most plausible explanation of my fears. Seize on it.

"I can discuss it with the others," Fabio motioned to the staff out by the monitors. "Probably it can be arranged."

I couldn't imagine it–shifting an operating day in America would be unthinkable.

"Thanks so much. Maybe if we could move it to Tuesday or Wednesday. . ."

"I'll try. Things are very flexible here."

Disease and family. Symptoms and sympathy. Perhaps a best way to judge a relationship would be to assess the attitudes toward illness by the two protagonists. The daughter of a doctor Alice grew up resenting illness–it always took Daddy away, cancelling vacation plans, abruptly ending fun family dinners, waking her up in the middle of the night to witness his required exit. And the phone brought only more demands. And if , God forbid, she herself became ill, why he could then compare her whining to the stoicism of his far more ill patients and lament her fragility, building her resentment even further. The son of an alcoholic, rule-ridden dysfunctional family I found, however, the magic release of illness. To be sick was to be given a reprieve from the elaborate, ritualized self-deception of the mess that was actual family life. To be ill was to receive some solicitation/recognition–one might even say, love–that was always plunged to the periphery (on the most distant slimy log) during the regular turn of each day. My sisters internalized the message so powerfully that they lived in illness and died early of lung cancer and brain tumors, addicted to pain killers and "treatments" of such appalling breadth and sweep as to take up every second of their lives.

In one of those moments of marital difference recognitions and consequent salvation we both pretended that nothing should upset original plans. I was recovering nicely. No need for a leap to Italy. Venetian medicine was first rate. Dr. Risica a savior par excellence. Let's harrumph and concede that nothing of import had happened. I would be getting my groin shaved because at some gut level it pleased and satiated my illness, the real illness quite beyond, above, greater, than the stupid arterial deposits. It is on such hard recognitions that marriages survive.

"Thanks for raising the possibility with them," I said to Fabio, who handed me the literary guide.

"Read the passage by Mann about the dangers of getting into a gondola."

"From *Death in Venice*?"

"Yes, I think so. It's terrific."

"Better than swapping phone chips?"

"No. Nothing's better than that."

"Students don't like it. I assigned it once in the preparation course, but they hated it. Instead they rented the Visconti film, which they hated even more. It takes more time to watch the film than read the story. I told them that but they hated both."

"Well, the passage is very good." Fabio said.

"I offered to give students a copy. Dover edition. I brought over six of them, but nobody took me up on the offer. I even said I'd take those who read it for lunch at the Des Bains hotel. But no response."

After Fabio left, I actually got out of bed to pee. The staff had to notice my violation of the rules but they seemed uninterested. I filled the plastic jug, eased back into bed and decided, after short while, that Mann's story had no relevance for my current situation. No red haired staff intruded on my stay, so death was not probable since Mann always dotted his narrative with red (usually red haired personnel) before calamity hit.

4.

Toward late Sunday afternoon, Tonio arrived carrying a pink Bic disposable razor. Short, stout, with two days growth of thick beard stubble, smiling. He held up the razor. "Time. Let's go."

"No shaving cream? " I said instinctively swiveling away from him.

"No. Don't need. Your triglycerides are lower than mine."

"So I get to shave you?"

"That's good. Let's go." He yanked down the draw string pajamas I had been issued–pale white with stag heads in blue, then pulled down my briefs. He began furiously to rake the Bic disposable across my upper stomach, working quickly down toward my groin. The scraping was terrifying. I put my hands over my genitals. He knocked them aside. "Don't worry. No danger." He said still scraping and scraping at ever increasing rates. "I do both sides–in case one side doesn't work so good."

"What?"

"Don't worry. It's quick."

His scraping seemed to escalate, get ever more furious as he got closer to my scrotum.

"Take it easy," I said trying to break his concentration.

"Don't worry," he answered, using a small square towel to buff away the hair. "I'm an expert at this. Don't worry."

He moved to the other side of the bed and began furiously again. He was like some squat threshing machine, sending out clouds of my pubic hair, the thigh pelt shearing, apparently thrilling to his productivity. As if frenzy itself would automatically rule out any possibility of sexuality in this grim ritual.

"Turn over," he said, wiping off the Bic.

"Why? He's not going to cut there. There's no reason–"

"The bandages maybe go all the way around."

More furious scraping . Could it be he was so fast, so savage because he loathed his job?

Would you want your privates shaved by someone who loathed the work? This work demeans me. I detest it. The more I do of it, the more I hate myself and you–if this were a straight razor I would have opted out of the work months ago and the hospital would still be paying the legal bills. It seemed his fury spewed out sentences such as these as I tensed against his slithering Bic.

"Done!" he shouted, "Pull up your pants."

"Thanks. You were terrific." I said sarcastically.

"People hate me. Americans especially. But when they pull off the bandages, you'll say what a good guy I am. Good guy. That's how you say it, right?"

"You're a really good guy," I answered.

Tonio cocked his head, smiled broadly. "Yours not so bad."

I wondered what "yours" referred to.

"Not so bad infarto. Maybe no angioplasty. No stints. You'll see. Dr. Risica thinks you can go home soon."

"Really?"

"Maybe. One thing—my tricylcerides lots higher than yours. I've got to stop that. Don't I?"

"Yeah. You've got to stop that."

"Maybe I don't have to. Maybe I can go on like this," he patted his massive stomach.

I said, "Why not die young and get it over with."

"Exactly!" he laughed. "We see things the same way."

"I don't think so. I wouldn't shave anybody."

"You would, if you were me. Believe me, you would."

Just before eight p.m. that night I saw Tonio at the monitors, bidding goodnight to the nurses who had just come on duty. He was wearing navy Bermuda shorts, socks and sandals and a tan T shirt pulled across that bulbous stomach. He was carrying a large plastic Coop bag filled apparently with his hospital garb and thick cushioned black shoes. And as he headed for the elevators he stopped off at my room and slid the door further back, for a wider view of the monitors. "Dr. Risica will see you tomorrow–he'll let you wait another day, if that's good for you."

"How do you know?"

"I know. Roberto, too. We know. That's all."

He turned around in my doorway and shouted to the staff beyond the monitors, "Ciao Tutti!"

And then turned down the hallway to the elevators.

After standing up once more to pee before 10 p.m. I eased back on to the thick muslin, and drifted into sleep, aided, perhaps, by the small white pill the night nurse brought at 9:30 p.m. I couldn't quite decide whether the enthusiasm of his "Ciao Tutti!" stemmed from his exit from the work and the hospital, or from his delight on being released from care and caring, or perhaps was only the expression of his child-delight in all his comrades. I sensed he was a kind of mascot on this third floor. Tonio, the frisky jolly wolverine.

Venice empties at night. The billion tourists flee to the train station or the car park and siphon off to cheaper digs on the mainland. There's only one campo near the University of Venice that even pretends to have a nightlife; the discos of the Mestre or across the top of the lagoon at Jesolo attract crowds who have spent the daylight in Venetian churches or museums. The empty streets and darkened buildings sculpt the clicking sound of the few foot steps along the stones. Those few centers of life in the city, Piazza San Marco, the Rialto bridge, Campo Santa Margarita appear only as light swirls beyond the shuttered buildings, pools of illumination in the far distance reflecting off the cloud banks overhead. And there is silence so elemental as to admit the sounds of the lapping canals on the slime covered Istrian stone of the buildings' foundations. In this darkened empty sound cavern the remaining Venetian is, on average, a woman over the age of sixty, living alone, each one a manque contessa. Since World War II the population of the city has dropped ; each year another 1500 leave, and contrary to all economic models, the price of housing in Venice goes up. "Ciao Tutti," indeed.

Around 12:30 a.m. I put another phone call through to Alice. I waited for the agonized cries of the old woman in the next room, but no sound came. Instead Alice and I talked as if we were across the dining room table in our house at home.

"People say I should fly over immediately, but Max has to be picked up and delivered. I don't know what to tell Roxanne about her visit."

"I think things should just go forward as usual."

Forward as usual—an interesting phrase. What is usual? Lying in "intensive care" Italian style somewhere between the Church of John and Paul and the cemetery of St. Michael?

"I actually feel quite good–very little pain, just lying here admiring the cleanliness, the unhurried care, the utter absence of stress in that care." Could the place be overstaffed?

"If it was because of stress that it happened, I want it understood that I wasn't there," Alice said. "I had nothing to do with it. If there was stress it came from someplace else."

"Point conceded."

"Good. Then I can say the doctors here think you're getting the right treatment. Drugs first then aggressive treatment if necessary."

"Aggressive?"

"Yes. First angioplasty, ballooning up the arteries, and then maybe whatever else is necessary, when they've run the dye and found the blockage."

"The dye?"

"They inject something in your blood and watch it on the television screen."

"Terrific."

"It's nothing. Supposed to feel very good in fact."

"Terrific."

"A hostile attitude only makes it worse," Alice says crisply.

"I'm not hostile. I'm bored. I'm scared."

"They say it's quite usual. Nothing to worry about. You can talk, you can move around, so the damage has been minimal."

I'm thinking, *minimal damage, forward as usual*–some link there. Maybe it's not the damage per se, but what the damage portends, suggests, illuminates. That long slimy green pole to oblivion with its surrounding warmth, light and billowy seductiveness. Our conversation drifts around the quotidian. What our youngest Laura wants for her birthday. Max's delights and dangers on the Cuban concert tour.

"I love hearing your voice." I tell Alice, and that stops the flow of words for a moment.

"You're not doing well." She answers.

"I'm doing fine–but my chest still hurts. Lot's less but still some hurt."

"You've told them that?"

"Yes, they know."

"Well, repeat that to them, will you?"

"Of course."

"Sometimes I sit here and I don't know what to do. What to think. What steps to take."

"You're doing fine. You've talked to the doctors there. That's the most you can do. I'm fine here. The food is quite good. The place is clean, modern. Brand new in fact. Dr. Risica is very positive. Let's just go ahead as if nothing really had upset things. You'll come over soon enough."

It seems another voice is speaking the line: *you'll come over soon enough.* A beckoning voice almost as beguiling as Alice's voice. Dulcet voice noting that cold water was inadequate for the task and Roberto's actions headed off the second slipping away, but there would come a third time and success at last.

"Laura insists there's nothing wrong and that you will be perfect again. She's absolutely certain of that in the most self-assured way. She's very convincing."

"Well, send her over."

"We'll all be there soon enough."

"Yeah, absolutely." I answered.

In the morning Dr. Risica and entourage arrived at 8:30, right after my porridge, and coffee.

"You want to delay the angiogram," he said in his distinctively gravel tones.

"Yes,"

"So your wife can arrive here?"

"Yes, probably, maybe not."

"Well, I have two more scheduled for tomorrow morning. So I can do yours before them.

First thing in the morning. You're still having pain in your chest?"

"Yes, but not much. Really not much at all."

"Tomorrow then, 8:30 ."

"I'm worried about the dye."

"Why?"

"Once when I had a kidney scan, they injected me with dye and a weird reaction set in. I started lumping up and turned red. They had to give me adrenalin."

Dr. Risica looked carefully at me. "When did this occur?"

"Oh, a long time ago. Twenty five years maybe."

"Well, we will prepare some special dye to minimize a reaction." He studied me a bit longer, making some calculation concerning my trustworthiness it seemed. I recalled the look the stranger fixes on Gustav Aschenbach in Mann's *Death in Venice*–a certain threatening recognition of perversion from a distance across the park in Munich before Aschenbach decides to take a spring break in Italy.

"It was a long time ago," I said, lamely.

"There have been many improvements," said one of his entourage.

"I'm sure," I answered.

There was a quiet, quick shuffle of Risica's sueded slippers and he disappeared to the right of the monitors. The rest of the entourage slowly wended out of the room. I wondered if I shouldn't have looked a bit more closely at Dr. Risica. Perhaps he was as old as the apparently youthful panama hatted fellow on the boat that brought Aschenbach to Venice. The reveler who couldn't hold his liquor despite being surrounded by youths willing to claim him as their own. Maybe his authoritative voice and swift manner masked a certain senility—only the hands were palsied, was that it? The hands that swizzled around the femoral artery of my right upper leg? Would Risica then show me the true abyss that Aschenbach lusted after? All over the gleaming steel of a castered table and tureens of blood?

Of course all that was nonsense. Fear musings from lack of language learning–dizzy extrapolations from translated German literature. Nothing of death happened in Mann's story unless something red strolled into the text–bow ties, or hair, or sashes, or crisp strawberries, lipstick. Red would out, and signal the end. Nothing red was anywhere at any time within the confines of the Ospedale Civile. I was sure of it, having looked carefully on each floor.

The last member of the entourage did not exit. He turned back from the doorway and drew a chair up beside my bed. He brought up a clipboard and spoke rather slowly as if English were not my native language, "Dr. Risica wanted me to explain a few things to you."

I forced a chuckle, "Of course. They don't ship bodies back, they ship only ashes and pulverized bones."

"Not quite," he answered unfazed . "It is important you understand the full option list before the angiogram begins. There are many steps–the angiogram is just the first one. If the test reveals nothing severe, the procedure stops. But if the test reveals blockages, then there are more steps to be taken. There is angioplasty, ballooning out the walls of the artery in question."

"The balloon is attached to the wire going through the artery?"

"It's not exactly a wire, a tube, and yes the balloon can be inflated from the tube and will be to expand the space in the artery. If that works to keep the artery open, then the procedure stops and you return to your room. But if the ballooning doesn't work then the third step is to put a stint into the artery right at the point where the artery is closing off, not holding out from the angioplasty. Do you understand?"

"Yes."

"But if the stint doesn't hold then the next step is a bypass surgery. So when I ask you to sign consent, you must understand you are agreeing to all the steps necessary to preserve the heart's full functioning."

"Do you do bypass surgeries here in Venice?"

"No. We would ship you over to Treviso or maybe Trieste.

"By boat?"

"Yes. By Boat. I personally don't think that will be the case with your test. I would be surprised even if we need to put a stint in; maybe even angioplasty won't be necessary. It will be revealed with the dye and the television screen. But to come back to the basic point.

If you sign, you agree to abide by the decision reached concerning your case."

"All the way through bypass surgery?"

"Yes," he answered apparently wearied by my belaboring the obvious. He was a beefy tall fellow, easily the biggest in the entourage. Was his selection to deliver consent forms deliberate? Who could refuse such a mountain of man? His green cap concealed all his hair, but his thick jowls had more than a little five o'clock shadow, and his forearms out from the green gown's sleeves had a Tonio-worthy density of black hair on their tops.

"All the way to Treviso ?" I asked again.

"Treviso or Trieste, I'm not sure which, but definitely not here. We don't do bypasses here."

Did it bother him that Venice, Lion Republic, empress of the world at one time, could not provide this routine service? I don't think so. Theme parks like history itself had limitations, despite Fabio's longings. No thick steaks and chops here on the sea shore. Take that defective heart and get yourself to the mainland, fella. The trees were numbered and labelled there, after all. He had soft eyes and for a moment I thought vaguely rouged cheeks, although I immediately decided I was remembering too much of Mann's story. It was Aschenbach who got his hair darkened to make himself look younger, more attractive to the beautiful boy Tadzio. This guy was no Tadzio. But he did have a disturbing sense of threat about him–somebody who could do me damage. A kind of Oscar of the Adriatic. A bit "dingy" in dulcet accented English.

5.

In the morning the red threats materialized. Two of them. Ugly muted reds, maroon dyed hair on the two lithe matrons who wheeled in the bed to Risica's operating room. I almost refused to roll over onto their castered coffin. Would they proffer strawberries? Aschenbach ate them and dribbled on his shirt, a signal the cholera would surely get him, if he hung around fetid Venice panting after beautiful Tadzio.

These women did not pant and their "red" hair had a metalic sheen, a wire density that struck me as singularly menacing–dried blood, was that it? Had they used their hair to clean off the hemorrhaging of the patient previously on the coffin slab?

The shorter one laughed a lot and said she had a special shot for me. "You will enjoy," she said, pushing up my T shirt sleeve.

So dual reds for this climactic moment–the footwomen of death. Where was Fabio, who had stopped by the previous night and assured me he'd be here first thing in the morning? They slid the steel door back and issued me out into the corridor, past the t.v. monitors, down the linoleum lined hall past fifteen doors. Then at the elevator I began to wooze.

"Ah, you enjoy the injection," she said flouncing her hair enough to reveal the dark roots.

"You dye your hair," I said to see what she'd respond.

"Of course," she answered immediately. "I'm a true red-head now!"

"It's very beautiful."

"Of course."

I remembered that in potentially stressful situations I should deep breathe, long belly-distending intakes of air and slow open-mouth exhalations, all the while focusing on some distant, inert point. In the operating room that point was the large monitor overhead to the left of the table they flipped me on.

"You enjoyed the ride, didn't you," she said, covering me with a fleece blanket. Then amid the regular clacketing sound she and her accomplice wheeled out their coffin. The monitor was a HP model and Fabio had remarked last night that HP made superb equipment, the best for these sorts of forays. Of course Venice would have the very best equipment. The oak trees in the Veneto had been numbered. I could imagine Fabio among them with a small laser burning the numerals in their thick bark, and entering their position from a GPS unit on his PDA for transfer back to the main frame at Venice

PART III: AT THE FALLS

University. Software tree selection, *Microsoft Tree*, available free with any purchase of a chainsaw beyond 21 inches in length.

Tadzio said softly—"Still looking at me, old man? Don't you know they're going to cut you and soon? They're going to put a tube right through the center of your heart and expand it so that you'll learn finally that love is so much bigger than your thoughts. So much more extensive than your shaved crotch."

"Incidentally," I answered him, "my students couldn't finish your story. Too boring, too tedious, too perverse. All that Greek myth crap. Not your fault," I added. "Everything else was your fault, but not that."

Tadzio swiveled on one foot, raised my fleece blanket.

"Ah, they didn't undress you," Roberto said, letting the blanket fall back down. "Take off the pants and underwear. I help. He's going in right there," pointing to the top of my right thigh.

"I know that." I answered, shedding clothing. "I know that. I understand that. You're not telling me anything I don't know."

The room took on a mint scent and the monitor came to life. I hoped for jiggling women but only the single grey dot suddenly swelled up. As if cued by the monitor my back suffused deeper into the cushioned coffin top, as care and consciousness eased away. Tadzio had waded out to the sandbar distant in the slate-grey Adriatic sea. Three bobbing masks directly overhead. Fleece blanket whisked away, replaced by a white sailcloth sheet with a large hole over my right thigh and groin.

"A small pain," said Dr. Risica in his distinctive green cap. A pinprick as if I had stepped on a sharp shell. "I'm in," Risica announced and there came a slithering noise. I was aware my thigh, my stomach, my chest, in turn was being chilled by some kind of very tiny serpent. The monitor blossomed to life in grey tone–a myriad of lines on the screen and one bulging a bit. "Now the dye." Risica announced in that wondrous basso profundo that resonated *competence, competence.*

All the masks above me turned to the screen. One of them pointed. There was nodding–apparent consensus. More slithering. "We've found the first blockage. I'm going to open it wider with the balloon and then we'll wait a minute to see if widening it works properly. If it stays open , that's all we'll have to do. If it closes down again, I'll put in a stint to keep it open. I'm opening the wall now. Please hold your breath."

With silken semi-delight I held my breath, conscious that by restraining myself I was entering the monitor overhead, becoming one with the lines.

"Breathe normally," Risica said somewhat louder, shattering the reverie.

"Stop breathing," he commanded again.

I was back in the monitor, aware that something momentous was about to happen. Something had to shatter. I was instantly transported to January 17, 1995 at 5:46 a.m. in Kobe, Japan. The endlessly solicitous Japanese had been characteristically thorough and implacable in their instructions: "earthquakes that caused side to side motion were easily endured; earthquakes that bounced buildings up and down, rather than side to side, were absolute murder, pure killers."

"In that case, pray for sway," I answered, proud of my alliteration.

My Japanese colleague at Kobe College for Women did not respond to this verbal offering, doubtless pondering it for some deeper meaning. Maybe the "pray" part led her astray.

In any event a jet engine roar from the center of the earth started at 5:46 and came howling up to the tatami on which I was asleep with my six year old daughter Laura. Alice was already up in the house's galley kitchen, preparing a streusel for the coffee cake she had promised Max and Emily upstairs the night before. Then the house lifted off its foundation, settled back down, lifted again and began a dribbling bouncing thunderous elevation/ de-elevation. The tatami room was surrounded by glass panels which shivered in the growing concatenation. Surely they would splinter across the room in another second. I scrambled quite conscious that this was a moment for simple heroics to cover Laura with my body. Ah yes, this would make a good story for her grandchildren–the moment Daddy saved me from flying glass. This is what good fathers always did–hurled themselves outward to smother the flames, procured the length of tube necessary to bring air to the daughter trapped underwater, anon shielded her body from the rocket propelled grenade by interposing his own stomach.

The artery on the screen suddenly belched outward, reaching unimaginable proportions, filling the screen with a bulge, as if it were a balloon just receiving 65 pounds of air pressure in less than a fifth of a second. My chest seemed exploding, the elephant tossed sky high, ball and board following upwards into the stratosphere, careening toward the sun, whipping past the moon, perhaps landing somewhere on the campo Giovanni et Paolo. Roberto yelled something.

Dr. Risica shouted, "Breathe normally. I'm sorry I forgot to say that sooner."

What did I care? The house was flailing up and down, up and down. The windows shuddering insanely. The scent of oil filled the room. Soon enough the gas space heaters would explode. Alice said later she slowly thought: *how sad I won't get to see the children again.* Her hands were full of butter and brown sugar and that smeared on the walls as the cabinets emptied, the plates rocketed out of the shelving, condiment bottles and brandy decanters smashed into each other in the descent to the coated floor.

"You're crushing me," Laura moaned.

"Mr. John! Mr. John! Are you there?" Roberto shouted again.

"You're lucky, you are." Oscar said.

And there was, again, that wondrous icy satisfaction with the disintegration rampant. So this is it, the tantamount event, the capstone experience, blowing up on the grey haze television screen beneath the HP sign of excellence, Fabio burning the trees with numerals. So swim over to the other side, friends. Save a daughter, lose a life. Is the scent mint or oil? The earth is full of petroleum aching to be let out, was that it? Pools of oil along the lead turned against the tide and held hostage until someone could gather the nets or funnels or pipings upward? Come out through the algaed wire mesh, Mr. John.

"Breathe normally."

"You're crushing me, Papa."

When the glass splinters you'll thank me. You'll thank me as we slide down the opening crevice to the center of the earth in the oil fumed sea already burning around our charred bones.

You can pick the slivers out of my back–will that make you feel more protected and loved? Instead the sea foamed and soared its oil scum surface backwards along the bow–the Adriatic churning as we skittered across to Trieste. There were two giant white cranes at the dock and a motorized gurney with green scrubs running along side. More gorgeously marbled hallways, and overhead halogen lights, a myriad masks. And Tonio leaning over, holding an oversize straight razor with BIC stamped on its side. "Say it!" he shouted.

"Say what?" I answered.

"Say it. You know it. Say it!"

"I don't know it."

"You know it. Say it. Say it loud. Say it now!"

Of course . Of course. I remembered: *Ciao Tutti*.

Cantankerous Trieste. What fascist leftover caused such argumentative fury in the city? Perhaps it's a product of the restless rebuilding constantly going on. The city is festooned with cranes and derricks, spearing up into the solid dull blue of the Adriatic sky as if to test the tear-strength of the atmosphere. What can be poked through? Yes, if the atmosphere is only a sheet pulled, yanked across the city so that fumigation or something can go on, then how much propulsion is needed to break through? How much thrust to sever the sailcloth and reach the sunlight backlighting everything? Only as much as comes spilling out of the mouths of each and every resident, no matter the station in life. Pure disputatiousness.

The two North Africans quarreled over who should throw the rope to the dock hands upon arrival. Then the dockhands refused to catch the rope which fell back into the Adriatic as if in disappointment. It took a hooked pole to bring the rope back aboard. Meanwhile the boat nicely coasted into the dock and one of the North Africans put an arm around the nearest dock pole. The other fellow jumped off with the rope trailing a brilliant spray of crystal droplets.

"You're like a damn dog," a dock hand shouted turning away from the spray as the North African sprinted by. "But I won't have dogs shaking filth on me."

"This dog is too good for you," came the lilting British accented response.

"The dog smells of urine and shit."

I was thinking, from the wooden cot that was slowly being hiked over onto the dock, there isn't a dog–why are they quarreling about a dog that isn't there?

"I will kill this dog."

"Not a chance," *and the North African pulled a knife.*

Abruptly three nurses and a very plump doctor came out of the shack on the dock.

"Please, please, please," *said the doctor.* "Can't you kill eachother after we get this fellow to the operating room. Time is precious here. Take a hand. Put away weapons and push this fellow along."

The North African took hold of the cot at the head and leaned in over me. "When we get inside I will slice him good. These Rumanians detest us."

I think I said, "Bypass me first."

The North African looked puzzled.

Bypass me first.

"Buy now? You want to buy a handbag now. Here? From this cot? I have several in the shack but we'd have to stop, and the silly doctor won't let me. Won't unless, of course, you ask him. Ask him! You can buy what you want. Even Alligator. But I still will slice him good. He fucks his own dog, can you believe it? He takes her from the rear like a dog himself. He ruffles her rump to get her hot; he splays out her paws on the lineoleum. She scampers to regain her footing. He slathers her with some kind of goo and he mounts her like the sick Spaniel he is. She howls at the penetration. He bays at the moon and in less than five squirmy thrusts consummation is achieved. That's what these people are, dog fuckers. They need slicing."

"No, no, I'm the one who needs slicing." I insisted. "I came here for that. I was brought here for that. So let's get to it."

"This gurney runs at nine miles an hour, tops. So we can only get to it at that rate."

"Not fast enough," the doctor said. "But as compensation we've bought a brand new, highly efficient rib spreader. It gleams in the O.R. Positively gleams."

"The Rialto Bridge sometimes gleams," I answered hopefully.

"Tourists seem to think so, but the garbage still lines the side canals and floats occasionally out under the bridge, so do the tossed, unsold flowers littering up the canal edges. And the scent of excrement is everywhere. It's worse than Tokyo. Sewer City. We used to call it Sewer City."

"Trieste faces the future squarely and resolutely with pride and aspiration. There are more cranes here now than in Shanghai. Think about it. More international hotels going up everyday. More office buildings, more apartment complexes, more contained malls. Trieste has the future by the throat. It's a perfect place to die in. You can sink into oblivion here all the while hearing the sounds of restoration taking place, the sounds of tomorrow's promise fulfilled. Expire here and learn the profound sanction of futility. The sweet nothingness of exploding possibility. Trieste will put three hungry wolverines inside your rib cage and then feed them slowly through your severed gut. And you can watch it all on your very own monitor complements of the Hewlett Packard Corporation. So come on by Trieste, hop the next boat to Trieste. Try Trieste and seethe! Writhe in Trieste, the last Italian bastion before Slavic descent. Trieste the truest gate against irrelevance!"

"Feeling blue? Go to Trieste, the jewel of the Adriatic. Something's always happening here."

"What is happening here?"

"Ah, you're being reconstructed here. The best of your thigh is going north to reconstitute your slumping heart. We're adding extra packets of sugar to your central engine so it can go on frothing milk in the mornings. Tireste got rid of its pastels years ago. Sand blasted them away. Got rid of its lilly whiteness in the sunlight. Tireste seeks out *metallic sheen colorations now. Only those. Shades of redness, maroons in the morning, vermillions at night, and in between erector set cranes etched in ochre. We'll give you a lovely little red bow tie for the top of your swimming suit and set you out on the sandbar of your choosing. If you're lucky you'll get to wear a Burger King Paper Crown, and Fabio will teach you MapInfo 9.0."*

"Is Fabio here?"

"Of course. He comes over every night to check on the construction and admire the HP monitors."

"Is he here now?"

"Is anyone here now? You've said it clearly: Ciao Tutti."

6.

Only when you can entirely let go, can you completely possess—or something like that. I was aware that at some point, after the fifth or the ninth, "Breathe normally," Dr. Risica turned me over to one of his massive-forearmed assistants. It was that stout, hairy fellow who inserted the second stint–the coil insuring easy blood flow. My fading away was not like the conscious energy-mounting rejection of the icy sea, nor was it like the conscious heroics of body repositioning. It was like nudging a cellar door open with your foot and feeling for just a second the cool draft from below, passing quickly by. Moist cool down there. The drop-away void. Downstairs to emptiness.

Back in the blue, stainless steel room, Roberto explained, "Your blood pressure collapsed again."

"So I was dead?"

"No. Not dead. Gone a little."

"Gone a little?"

"Not dead. What did you feel?"

"A breeze."

"Wind?"

"Yes. My daughter said I was too heavy."

Roberto leaned against the blue wall. "Okay," he said.

"And I couldn't get my leg around the log."

"Okay."

I was thinking, Roberto doesn't speak much English. "And my classmates were laughing at my language. But did I go to Trieste?"

"No," Roberto laughed. "Not Trieste. Only back here."

"Everything is over then. Done?"

"Yes."

"No reason to go to Trieste?"

"No reason. No need."

"I wasn't on a boat?"

"No. No boat."

"And my leg is in tact?"

"The leg is fine. A bandage at the groin. You can feel it, can't you?" Roberto pushed on the mound of gauze taped at the intersection of my right thigh and lower stomach. "There a roll of bandage pushing down on your cut. Tomorrow I will come and take the bandage away and you can leave the hospital, if we can get the bleeding to stop."

"What bleeding?"

"After I take the bandage off. It takes my pushing on the cut to shut it down."

"Pushing?"

"With my fist, testing to make sure the cut isn't opening up."

"With your fist?"

"This one." Roberto holds up his right fist. "I push and release and then the cut closes."

"How long does it take?"

"Maybe one hour. I push and release a lot and soon it stops."

"I can't wait."

"You have to. It's tomorrow, after things are healing."

When, after ten thirty, Fabio arrived I explained to him this peculiar ritual–Roberto's fist on my slivered femoral artery. Was this standard procedure? Fabio didn't know. Didn't care.

"It must be usual," Fabio said.

"Usual, right into rupture," I answered. "Aschenbach gets to die comfortably in his chair, watching the sea, wrapped in his blanket. I get to be ruptured in the name of healing."

"I don't think so. But you can probably imagine it that way. Does that help you?"

"I keep getting phone calls for you."

Fabio laughed. "Of course, the chip is my phone in yours. What do you say to them?"

"I don't speak Italian. What do you think I say?"

"Just say, 'Not here.' Ciao."

"Dr. Risica says they've made a CD of the whole procedure."

Fabio perks up wondrously. "A CD?"

"Yes. He'll give me a copy tomorrow some time."

"A CD," Fabio repeats. "That's fantastic. That's like the cherry on top of the cake. I bet nowhere in the U.S. could you get a CD of what they've done. A CD of everything." It is as if his vision of the Veneto and the future has been validated. "That's fantastic! Amazing."

Would Aschenbach have been content with J-Peg images of Tadzio on his own CD, with streaming video to replace the figure out in the surf–the lad looking back seductively? And I was thinking, of course the Venetians would make superb records of their work–wasn't the whole historical profession for a while persuaded that the Venetian diplomats' records were infallible representations of the way the world truly was? I would have my own CD of the process, so that if chest pains commenced again, I could carry my CD and show it to the rest of the stultified cardiac treatment universe. They surely would have genuflected to the Veneto's technological superiority. And Fabio would get a chance to eat the cake's improbable cherry, juicy red bits dribbling on his beige polo shirt.

"What am I going to talk to Roberto about when he's pushing–. Excuse me–*intermittently pushing* on my groin?"

"You don't have to talk." Fabio answered. "Maybe you could get him to play the CD."

"Of course. We could watch it together. Have popcorn and maybe neck a bit. Maybe Roberto is Tadzio. Is he beautiful? A regular Greek statue, with his hair curling over his ears and down his neck, and," I picked up the collection Fabio had given me, and quickly found the passage from Mann's story, "and 'The laces bows and embroidery on his English sailor suit, with its puffy sleeves that narrowed below and closed tightly around the delicate wrists of his still childlike but slim hands gave his delicate figure a rich and pampered appearance.' Yes, of course, rich and pampered Roberto. Not exactly fourteen, however, or terribly thin."

"Maybe he's read the story," Fabio offered.

"Wanna bet?"

"Did they give you anesthesia?" Fabio answered.

"No. A little valium I suspect in the shot before the angio."

"I'm sorry I didn't get here in time to walk you in. But you seem to be fine now."

"Not a problem. You have to go through these things alone. That's clear. I didn't mind that."

"Well, I'll come back tomorrow around five and take you home, if everything's okay. They seem to think it's fine–Dr. Risica used the term 'optimale' regarding the results of the angioplasty and stints."

"So long as they don't clot, everything will be aces, I guess." I said.

"There are some drugs you have to take. We can pick them later, after you get home."

The rest of the afternoon was given over to proving my bowels were capably regular, utilizing a wheeled portable toilet chair brought into the room. I was to produce but not to strain, lest the wound open. One of the dyed red haired nurses validated my efforts. Otherwise I was to lay motionless on the bed and allow the artery to seal over. The roll of gauze clamped over the cut apparently kept the fused healing on-going. There was a steady ache to the pressure of the bandage, and most of the day remaining I drifted in and out of semi-sleep, aided, no doubt, by the small white pill one of the redheads brought with a very flexible paper cup.

Some time after midnight I tried to use the plastic pitcher for micturation, laying it on my stomach and releasing against gravity, but the pitcher filled and slopped onto my chest soaking the T shirt. I lay in heat and then chill and stench of urine and self-pity. So this was the essence of exit, I thought, not clambering aboard a slimy log, not sheltering your progeny against the hurts of the this world, but merely the lonely chill of piss in the night rising like a tide against your breathing, and the hum of HP machinery, and woman moaning in the next room, and Mann brooding about the discipline of art succumbing to the swills of emotion, the frenzy of sudden libido driving all before it. Not even that, just the sappy tiredness of being unable to sit up or loosen an angry ache in the right crotch. How I wanted, suddenly, to bat away the hard roll of gauze strapped to my leg and stomach.

In wet despair I called Alice and for forty minutes we talked about the difficulties of getting Max's bass in its giant coffin like container to the airport for shipment to Cuba, about Emily's attempts to fly in from Kazakhstan, about Laura's eyeliner and penchant for denim, about the endless rain in New England and the sudden cold, about the specials at Shaw's supermarket, and about Sonny Karotis's failure to win the primary to the Worcester city council. Alice signed off with a careful, "It's been great sitting behind you in Algebra II."

Roberto arrived at 10:20 a.m. "Now I must start to push against you. But first you must change your shirt." He came back with a bowl and some hot water and a small towel. He cranked the bed up and I swabbed off, put on a new T shirt. He cranked the bed flat again, slipped the pajama bottoms down and eased the adhesive straps off the gauze. He folded in four a small fluffy towel and rested it over the cut. He stopped and lowered the entire bed. "Now we begin," he said, gently pushing on the folded towel.

"Do you live in Venice," I asked.

"No. Near Padua."

"Why not Venice."

"Too expensive. No one in the hospital can live in Venice. No one. Rents too high in Venice." He pushed down hard and an ache blossomed out from his fist. He eased off. I rubbed my eyes. How much can realty issues occupy the time? More pushing. More pain. Then easing. Then pain. Then easing.

"Do you drink spritzes?" I asked.

"Yes. Of course."

"With Aperol or Compari?"

"Con Aperol, of course."

A Venetian spritz is unknown outside of Venice- a mix of white wine, lemon squeeze, Aperol (a peculiar apple liquor with a magical orange color) and sparkling water. You'd think a lemon peel twist would be the likely decoration but Venetians add a solid green olive on a toothpick. Roberto explained he added two olives. If his shift ended in the early afternoon he sometimes stayed at a bar in the campo until 9:30 p.m., drinking spritzes.

The Aperol gives the drink a reflected orange watery color that undulates in the sunlight much like the canals themselves, and in the heat the alcohol mix carries a soft punch, loosening appreciation for the soft air and occasional salt haze of Venice. The orange scent also masks any sewer smell in the area.

Twenty minutes into the push/ease routine I've learned that Roberto has a two year old son who sleeps fitfully. That he'd like to live in Venice as would most of the hospital workers–they all hate the commute through Ferro Via and the outside line–but because everyone wants to own some small portion of Venice, apartments spiral upward in cost and rent, even though acres of buildings are unoccupied. The realtors wait quietly for the myriad elderly women living alone in the flats to pass away, so that their relatives can turn the building into enormous cash. And the specialist rehabilitators can overcharge for meticulous restorations, so that elites from Rome and Milan can point to their Venetian holdings. "And they are just holdings. Just holdings," Roberto emphasizes. "Holding on for a visit maybe twice or three times a year."

"But I see school children sometimes."

"Only in Duseduro and Carrnaregio–nowhere else. Maybe St. Elena–just the rich remote places in Venice." Roberto answers.

PART III: AT THE FALLS

More pushing and easing off. Some blood appearing on the edge of the towel.

"My wife mentioned in America they use sandbags to put constant pressure on the cut," I said after a while.

"In Trieste we have some clamp machines. We do that sometimes but with older people, this is a better method."

"I suppose I am older."

"I meant very older."

"I see."

"We are making good progress," Roberto says.

"I wonder."

"No, good progress. I will be able to stop soon. Less blood. Almost nothing now."

"Nothing but the ache," I answered.

"It's a healing. A good healing."

"Worth several spritzes. I promise to buy you some after I get out."

"That's good."

Empty promise, I think. I will go home to America and the clotting coil will kill me before I could come back for spritzes. Roberto probably knows that.

"My wife wants to move closer to Venice. To Mestre where you can get some cheaper apartments, but it's dirty there. Industrial. I don't like it in Mestre."

"You been to the Panorama there?"

"Yes, of course."

"My students discovered it and the free bus to it from Venice. Their idea of a proper supermarket, with a few strange touches. The horsemeat section, for example. But everything is out in the open, grabable. It makes them very happy to visit a familiar supermarket. They get tired of asking for everything. They prefer to pick their own."

"Help yourself," Roberto says as verification of the sentiment.

"Right. Help yourself. Do it yourself. That's the American way."

"Except for stints," Roberto says.

"What do you mean?"

"Dr. Risica is very good. That's what I mean."

"I don't think so. I think you meant something else."

He stops pushing for a moment, appears to consider the idea and then repeats, "No, that's what I was thinking."

To cover, after a few moments, I ask, "What do you buy at Panorama?"

"Ties. They're very good buy there."

"Ties?"

"Yes."

"The students were surprised to find a horsemeat section in Panorama."

"It's not surprising."

"You eat horsemeat?"

"Sometimes."

We have exhausted the topic. Each time he pushes, I sit up a bit, then fall back. Starting to sit up eases the discomfort.

"No blood this time," Roberto says.

"So we're done?"

"No another ten minutes , perhaps."

"You play tennis?"

"No. Do you?"

"I used to. Now I'm not so sure."

Light through the narrow windows at the top of the wall grew brighter. Venetian haze lifting.

I was lifting too, bouncing slightly upward with each fist push.

"This has to be the most retro treatment ever," I said, getting more uncomfortable.

"Retro?"

"Backward, from the past, from some other time when they didn't know what they were doing."

Was that going too far?

"Yes, but it works very well. You'll see. In a month no one will be able to find where Dr. Risica cut."

"My skin will be blemishless, when I die of another heart attack, is that it?"

Part III: At the Falls

"Yes. You will be without a scar." Roberto said without a trace of sarcasm or ill feeling. A simple declaration of flawless surgical care.

The narrow panes above grew lighter still, as if in exclamation of his point.

At last he put a large bandaid over the spot. He smiled at me. "Don't move too much for a while. And then everything will be perfect." He gathered up his small towel.

"Thanks, I guess." I answered.

"Yes. It will be perfect. Perfecto." Roberto said as he left.

I thought but didn't say, that's what waiters say when you finally figure out what to order off the inscrutable menu.

One of the dyed red women brought lunch and later the pottie chair. I dozed most of the afternoon until Fabio woke me around five o'clock.

"We can leave," he said. "I think the vaporetto to Ferro Via and then down the Grand Canal is the shortest, smoothest route."

"Can't we run the addresses and the program to get a map."

"It's not funny."

"I thought I'd have to bicycle or something to prove I'm okay."

"No, they won't ask that for another month when you come back for a check-up. I have your prescriptions–a lot of them. We can go now."

"Just like that? No bill?"

"I don't think there will be a bill. This is Italy. Medicine is taken care of here."

"They took my insurance card and xeroxed it."

"But I don't think they will invoice you."

"Flexible scheduling for angioplasty and no bill. I don't understand it."

"It's Italy. Medicine is free here."

"I don't think so."

"Well, you'll see eventually. Anyway nobody will stop us leaving, and you're going back to the U.S. before a month anyway."

"I will need my records."

"I'll get them later, next week. That will cost some money. And so will the drugs. But I already have," Fabio gleefully smiled and cocked his head, "the CD–right here. Dr. Risica handed it to me on the way up here."

"The cherry on the cake."

"Yes. Absolutely. Way ahead of the U.S. in these matters."

"My data base of coronary artery disease. Is it in Access?"

"Streaming video," Fabio answered. "All the software needed to open it is already on the disk. It's perfectly self-contained."

"Like you."

"Yes, of course." Fabio said.

We took an older, smaller vaporetto. We sat up front inside, below the water line. The windows steamed, even though they had been cranked open. It was close and hot inside. My arms were bruised from the blood tests and IVs. "You look like a drug addict," Fabio said, noticing that other passengers were staring at us.

The air in the boat was soft and mucid and full of Venetian light, a steamy but welcoming experience. We changed boats at the station, and went two stops to San Stae. It was a long walk to the campo and twice I had to rest against a building but I was heartened to realize I could eventually complete the walk to the apartment, without any chest pain.

I sat on the couch again, looked at the vaguely slavic family photographs; Fabio went to the co-op and brought back some eggs and bread, and a bottle of Pepsi. I reassured him I would be fine, especially with his own cell phone.

"How do I thank you for all this help?" I said.

"You get well and we finish the projects," Fabio answered. "But don't worry about them. I can finish them easily. I'm used to doing that, you know."

"I know that well enough."

"So just get well. I will call later." And Fabio went back out through the courtyard.

About 8:30, there was a knock at the door and I let Mrs. Deste in. We looked at each other a bit puzzled and then she sat down on

Part III: At the Falls

the small chair opposite my couch. We were perched in the same positions five days ago. And there was the same language-strangled awkwardness. Was she disappointed I had come back to reclaim the apartment? It didn't seem so. She leaned in off her chair a bit and stared at me in a penetrating way, as if to discover something inside my chest.

Maybe she was worried about her own health, I decided. So I started talking in what I thought was a reassuring way.

"I'm fine now. And thank you so much for coming over to check on me, not only now but before. That's very kind of you. It takes something like this to make you realize how kind most people are, how helpful they want to be." I leaned forward myself as if testing whether she followed that little burst of English. She pulled back a bit and said, as if directed: "Yes. Yes. Yes."

"I appreciate your kindness," I went on. "Especially since I don't really understand what has happened. I wish I had a clear sense of what went on, what is going on. What it means. That's what's so peculiar, the sense that it's just happening and I'm a kind of side actor experiencing the event, though that's too weighty a word. Look, it's not about Alaska, is it? It's not about almost drowning–not even a little bit. And it's now about saving little Laura from flying glass, is it? Is it?"

"Yes. Yes, yes." said Mrs. Deste.

"It's about what went into those happenings–it's about horse-meat sections in a super supermarket and expensive rents in Venice and getting shaved in odd places, and going or not going to Trieste."

"Trieste. Yes." Mrs. Deste said.

"We had a project that was supposed to help ambulance boats finding the shortest route to anyplace in Venice, for speedy recovery, for saving Venetians from death, but the project didn't work because the software wasn't needed. It's like a record of something that doesn't mean anything, a guide post to nowhere, a map of water flowing. And Fabio thought it was going to be fabulous and put the Veneto back on the map, so to speak. But it didn't, did it?"

"Yes." Mrs. Deste said tentatively.

"It's about spritzes made with two olives and maybe kinds of grappa sold at someplace north of here, maybe Bassano."

"Bassano, yes." Mrs. Deste said.

"I want to thank you for being so wonderful and caring and for coming over here. I don't think you came to check on the real estate. I don't believe that. I look into your eyes and I see kindness and the things I think about when I talk to my family who are so far away and I'm alone here, except you're here, too and that's . . .that's very kind. But I was thinking a couple of days ago, I was thinking about the earthquake in Kobe. You know it killed over 6500 people. I was thinking the night before the earthquake the dog next door didn't make his crazy howl. Every night about nine o'clock he howled. A really unearthly howl, the kind of prolonged scream you expect a retarded child of ten or so to make if you pulled off one of his arms. But the night before the quake the dog didn't howl. They put him outside and he didn't howl, and all night long I heard ravens landing on the roof tiles, lots of them. Maybe two or three hundred of them. But I still didn't have a clue, didn't have even an inkling that something was awry. But I did lie awake on the futon for a while and I thought, I wonder why the dog didn't howl. But then I fell asleep and later my youngest daughter came downstairs and joined us on the tatami mats. They're so comfortable you can lie down anywhere, even without a futon and fall asleep and they smell so much better than Venice. So much better. And I didn't go to Trieste. At least I think I didn't. Dr. Risica uncorked the pain and the elephant went away. Off to Jesolo."

Mrs. Deste got up and still leaning forward came across the room to me. She peered down at me and smiled and said slowly, as if to emphasize the syllables and therefore make the word clear and communicative:

"Infarto?"

I looked away from her face, stared down, rather, at the gleaming and chill marble spreading out through my socks and said, "Si, infarto."

www.ingramcontent.com/pod-product-compliance
Lightning Source LLC
Chambersburg PA
CBHW071444150426
43191CB00008B/1232